THE LOVES OF

Ricardo

Ricardo
Sánchez

TIA CHUCHA
PRESS

Some of the poems have appeared in the following books bearing Ricardo Sánchez' copyright: *Canto y grito mi liberación* (1973), *HechizoSpells* (1976), *Milhuas Blues and Gritos Norteños* (1978), *Eagle-Visioned/Feathered Adobes* (1981), and *Amsterdam Cantos y Poemas Pistos* (1983).

Poems that come from collections or anthologies: "Vision" from *We are Chicanos: Anthology of Mexican American Literature*, ed. Phillip D. Ortego; "y from here, where?" from *Erlanger Studien, Band* 65/1, ed. Wolfgang Binder.

"Festival of Children" and "I Know You by Your Smile-Filled Songs, Chinto" were first published in *Selected Poems by Ricardo Sánchez* (Houston: Arte Público Press, U. of Houston, 1985).

Poems published in journals include: "as we walk" and "the door is open" from "Questions: Moot/Salient or Refractions," *Touchstone* 8.2 (1983); "raza mindsouls," *De Colores: Journal of Chicano Expression and Thought* 3.1 (1976); "con amor y cariño," *New Blood* 6 (April 1982); "convicts, inmates, & felons too," *Lemon Creek Gold: A Journal of Prison Literature* 1 (Fall 1979).

The remainder of the poems in this collection have previously been unpublished.

Thanks to M.S. Hetherington for her vision and hard work, and to Sandra Cisneros and Luis Rodriguez for their generous support.

This project is partially funded by grants from the National Endowment for the Arts, the Illinois Arts Council, and the Eric Mathieu King Fund of the Academy of American Poets.

Printed in the United States of America.

ISBN 1-882688-14-7
Library of Congress Number: 96-62082

Book design: Jane Brunette
Cover concept, cover painting, and title page illustration: Chista Cantú
Back cover photo: Rikárd-Sergei Sánchez
Editorial assistance: Mary Hawley, Mark Ingebretsen

PUBLISHED BY:
Tia Chucha Press
A Project of the Guild Complex
P.O. Box 476969
Chicago, IL 60647

DISTRIBUTED BY:
Northwestern University Press
Chicago Distribution Center
11030 S. Langley
Chicago, IL 60628

CONTENTS

INTRODUCTION

Ricardo Sánchez was most widely known for his social activism and for poems that reflected anger against the actions of American society toward Chicanos and other underrepresented groups. His early works, such as *Canto y grito mi liberacion* (1971) and *HECHIZOspells* (1976), though multifaceted, reverberate wrath. Thus, a book entitled *The Loves of Ricardo* might seem like a contradiction. But Sánchez's public persona was misunderstood. In our contemporary "talk show" world, where the word "love" is thrown about so profusely, few really understand what it implies. For Sánchez, love was a celebration of life in its fundamental aspects. Love is what his life revolved around.

During his life, Sánchez was involved in many cultural and political causes and clashed with many people. His keen intellect and his love of and ability to use words effectively reinforced his impulse to lash out the instant he sensed falsity. He did not shy away from expressing his thoughts in his poems, notes, or newspaper columns written for San Antonio and El Paso dailies, and he disregarded the effect that these words might have on other people or on his career as a writer.

Sánchez's abilities as a public orator were unique and frequently in demand. He was robust and tough, and had a stern and piercing gaze. His voice was a low, melodic, hypnotizing thunder that showered words of rage and bliss simultaneously. The passion, power, and eloquence of his speeches and performances made him a person to be respected.

Though Sánchez was serious in his beliefs, he was playful with words. Words were his toys, and he enjoyed creating playful images and parodies of people. This playfulness, known as *cábula*, often confused the uninitiated and made some people feel that they were being attacked or ridiculed.

Consequently, some saw him as too uncouth and too tempered by barrio and prison harshness. They believed he was too difficult, too explosive, and too dangerous to deal with. For some, then, it may be difficult to associate Sánchez with love.

Nevertheless, to the many people who got to know Sánchez on a personal level, the contradictions soon vanished. One could see the tenderness and gentleness with which he treated his wife, his children, his friends, and even strangers. Many were shocked that this could be the same man who wrote his early works of rage.

I knew Sánchez for more than twenty years. Though he moved and lived in many areas of the United States and I remained in El Paso, we kept in contact. Every time he came into town we would pick up our discussion where we had left off months before. When, for family reasons, he moved back to El Paso in 1988, I got to know Sánchez much better. For three years prior to his leaving to teach at Washington State University, we engaged almost daily in marathons of dialogues and arguments.

From this vantage point, I was able to witness the many private and public sides of Sánchez: the husband, the father, the friend, the poet, the spokesman, the performer. All of these aspects revolved around one theme—love. Not love in the sense of trying to fill an emptiness by creating and using dependence on another, but love as a celebration of one's strength as a human being.

Paradoxically, he was continuously misinterpreted by opposite perspectives. Though he had achieved tenure at Washington State University while teaching in both the English Department and the Department of Comparative Cultures, he had been rejected by the academic world of the Southwest. Perhaps associating him with his *pinto* (convict) background, his fellow professors felt that he was too harsh and unrefined. Yet, he commented, when he read his love poetry at Chicano community activist gatherings, he would sometimes be labeled as "wishy-washy" and too refined.

This paradox has much to do with the essence of this book—a misunderstanding of what love is and a struggle to understand it. Social philosopher and psychoanalyst Erich Fromm states that when humans evolved from a communal to a marketplace orientation, material progress occurred at the cost of deteriorating authentic human relationships. In the competitive universe, according to Fromm, we tend to sell our personalities as commodities or services. Therefore, to be successful requires adopting a pleasing personality and any other attributes necessary for a particular position. The market will decide if these qualities are useful. Thus, one's self-worth depends on what others think. This frame of mind leads to a misuse of love; that is, it eventually leads to a kind of false love that is based on manipulation and power.

Domination and discrimination in contemporary society, Fromm said, is a result of the lack of genuine love. Though humans have a basic need to transcend themselves and relate to others, this relating has been subtlety and effectively disfigured by society's marketplace orientation, in which people can only relate to each other as objects.

Sánchez grew to understand that a society that lacked an understanding of love would base its human relationships on power and domination. Meaning and progress meant having power and dominion over nature and other beings. He cried out against such false normalcy because these conditions could not allow human beings to actualize themselves to their full potential. The reflection of his experiences as a Chicano lead him to abhor this pattern of power and domination.

Sánchez stated that he was not searching for power, because he didn't need or want to have power over anyone else. What he demanded, though, was strength. Strength gave the individual the capacity to defend himself or herself against subjugation and victimization. With this virtue, individuals could express themselves on equal terms as self-actualizing human beings. In a poem to his newly born daughter, Sánchez writes:

> Who'll be free, with inner peace
> that you'll never bow nor cringe,
> that you'll share in liberty,
> ever knowing who you are,
> ever proud of where you've come,
> That you'll never feel inferior
> nor superior, Libertad

Similarly, in his Les Suerostraats notes ("There is only the open door . . ." - 1988) he states:

> no, I do not want to own you nor can I, my power is
> too fragile and too evanescent to pretend that you

are less or that you can fit in my pocket besides
my cigarette pack: you too are a giant, an
amorphous being of many silhouettes and nuances,
and I cannot possibly fit in your pocketbook.

Sánchez's love and celebration of differences is echoed throughout the great majority of his love poems. His appreciation and love of differences can be traced back to his upbringing in El Paso, Texas, a city on the border with Mexico where two different histories and consciousnesses are juxtaposed—near yet far apart. Before Hispanicization, the Chicano, for the most part—not the Mexican or the American—had been the group that had been able to internalize both world views. Ignored by both worlds, the Chicano reacted against the dominating tendencies of both worlds, for their juxtaposition allowed them to have contact with both on a daily basis.

Eventually gang-like groups of young people called *pachucos* developed. They expressed an existential reaction to the fact that they could not identify with and felt forgotten by both American and Mexican culture. Theirs was a natural phenomenon, not an intellectualized one. They took up gang-like activities, a unique style of dress, and a dialect known as *caló* that combined idiomatic phrases of English and Spanish. Thus, Sánchez's poetry is rife with neologisms, metonymy, and metaphors, just as *caló* is.

The Chicano was a decentered being, not adhering to any culture that emanated from a center such as Mexico City or Washington, D.C. American sociologists could only describe the Chicano as an unacculturated ethnic group still clinging to Mexican culture and language. From the Mexican perspective, intellectuals such as poet Octavio Paz could only describe the Chicano as a fractured Mexican.

Sánchez rejoiced in this difference, in this differing. He felt the term Hispanic de-emphasized the Indian roots of the Chicano and took away the mestizaje or blending aspect. Furthermore, the synthesis of the Chicano essence went beyond the mixture of Spanish and Indian. It also included the Moorish, Sephardic, Germanic, and Roman background of Spain as well as cultural—and at times blood—mixtures of the North American dynamic: Northern European, Jewish, African, and Asian.

Though Sánchez was essentially a universalist, he believed that the best way he could express his cosmic consciousness was from a Chicano perspective. He loved his Chicanoness, and he believed that this self-love needed to be expressed and shared. He believed that his people (*raza*) needed to understand their roots, and that this search had to be authentic, not one of self-aggrandizement. A genuine search would require that the individual learn to have a productive love based on thought, feeling, and action—not a love based on power or that sought recompense. Simply, a love where sharing, empathy, and the celebration of the individual uniqueness and potentiality of each person is expressed. As the search for roots proceeds and merges with the search for love, a person doesn't lock himself or herself into his or her own culture; rather, the opposite occurs. As barriers are broken, the Chicano—just as any other group member in the world—will understand that we are all one.

The Loves of Ricardo is an attempt to put some of Sánchez's poems dealing with love into chronological order. Many of these were written in notebooks and dated, almost like journal entries, and are published in this volume for the first time. Throughout the book, the reader will see different dimensions of love—marital love, paternal love, familial love, fraternal love, communal love (*raza*), aesthetic love, and universal love. Dividing these poems into separate thematic sections would have been one way, perhaps more reader-friendly, of organizing this book. But as one reads the poems—including those that may be addressed to his beloved wife, María Teresa or to his children, Rikárd-Sergei, Libertad-Yvonne, or Jacinto-Temilotzín—one begins to see that any one poem can contain other elements of Sánchez's search for, and sharing of, love.

Roberto Barcena
El Paso, Texas
March, 1997

Tap, Tap, Tap

tap, tap, tap . . .
again do your heels tap;
their resonance
           echoing,
           reverberating
from wall to wall,
mockingly manifesting
your inner savagery . . . .

rap   rap   rappity rap . . .
fiery fingers
manipulating castanets,
madly proclaiming
           your artistry!
your just-born-in-the-jungle eyes
betray your wanton-ness!
yes,
glide
      away
swiftly,
let your audience
         go home,
o,
so hungry,
desperately desiring you . . .

you're being betrayed,
though,
BY YOUR EYES . . .
eyes, without comparison,
eyes that tell,
nay, that shout
your secret loathing . . .
for the multitudes!

sadly it is,
your tomorrows
            shall have less flowers
than your yesterdays . . .

like all women,
you were born to die
and
dying shall leave you
            dessicated,
devoid of soul
            too soon!

Evening in Prison:
Theme & Variated Vibrations—
Beethoven's Quartet
in C Sharp Minor/Strings

amid crescendos of conviviality,
betwixt softness and strains of peace,
       inaugurable tintinnabulations lilt out
       muted love calls from my famine/weak esprit . . .

it is a night of pure remembrance
hailed by the euphony of strings—
       & i can only mentally galavant
       to other star-struck nights
when you were the all-engulfing warmth
and your pulse the beat,
       your words the structured melody
       and your rhapsodic sighs
the finale to our own composition;

Dearest, someday,
       we shall again hear
       Beethoven and
we shall be enraptured;
our love shall keep time
to strings at evening hues and
       burst forth crescendos . .
Beloved, concertos and love toasts
enlace us, bind us;
       we are enwebbed cocoon-like
       in the caressing wool music/love is . . .
Virtuosos—rabin & horowitz—lull out
symphonic overtures
       that haloize you,
       and lovingly

do i see you palpitate
depth and totality
             with love's musicality
             complementing you . . .
tonight soft sounds shall emanate
and flood my thought world,
          again i shall behold you
          in the furtiveness of hope . . .

Rik-Ser:
my progeny

Rik-Ser,
last weekend
you hurt . . .
and cried
feeling the sting
discipline is . . .
and
you wanted then
to exact revenge

yet
later relented
wishing to make up;
you followed me
everywhere,
your tender hands
held mine
caressingly;

then and there
I saw your utter soulfulness,
loved you more articulately
than
I could
previously
conceive . . .

Rik-Ser,
your eyes reflect
visions now lost to me . . .

for youth is wise sensitivity
till
we (older) fools
annihilate it,
and
I know
our relationship
stifles you . . .
even though
I try
I cannot feel
the shooting rays
hope, joy, & life are
to
young, sensitive souls . . .

out / parole
the fan/Richmond, Virginny
Frederick Douglass
Journalism fellow, 1969

—hijo—

I give you
the turbulence
being Chicano is,
I give you
the feeling
loneliness is . . .
for you must combat, hijo,
life your own way,
so i teach you
what it can be
to be yourself . . .
it is a hurting kind of life
when you are different
or considered different,
even though
you are just
as
human
as
the neighbor next door . . .

Rikard,
your needs
come on strong & pungent
and the whiplash
of your desires
invades my every moment; i, too,
was young, vibrant, yet angry but loving
  (and now am old & bitter/angry)
and

society
had
a cure that did not work
or magically change me . . .

you are vortex & matrix
and the dichotomy of being
the new Chicano . . .
and
at night
i view you
in sleep's sanctuary—safe
for this moment, but tomorrow:
what?
      only
          more
              of
                the
                    same?
damn, but i surely hope not,
that's why we struggle for la causa.

Teresa

in the midst of our pobreza
we bask in each other's arms,
your warm, tender brown-ness
calms the pandemonium in my loins;
lost within the downy joyous wellspring
nestled in the soul's thigh lining,
you murmur of creation
as our beings fuse in love,
and your being glows aborning
our next child's loved gestation;

> it is good, Teresa,
> just being/sharing,
> and a long time ago
> while imprisoned
> i felt/imagined
> the lunacy of last night's loneliness
> and recalled/hoped:
> > "nights explode conundrums and pensées,
> > days obliterate mordicant somberness
> > > (and somehow all this is relegated
> > > to a nightmarish closet in my mind),

> projections to a bright tomorrow
> flood every waking moment
> > like a facade for today's harsh reality,
> and the soul weeps its tormented lament
> homesick for a past turned bizarrely beautiful . . .
> and negates now the soul
> > a garish and unsane present.
> Hungrily comes the surging yen,

for tomorrow's oft promised, never yielded
well of fulfillment—and the mind
    (there is awareness of self) kens
an abstraction of multifaceted self-deceptions
    (yours? mine? THE WORLD'S!) and shudders out
its gasp of resignation,
    even though the cry
'I LOVE YOU, DEAREST TERESA!'
    lingers on
amidst the barren steel of walls/bars/&
    tenderless nights,
    and hope fights on implacably. . . . "

we've turned the tide around,
nestled our realities
within the coverlets of love,
and soon another voice shall sing
its soft melodic tunes
and gird us with a smile. . . .

Son: my love destroys you slowly

fire, need, and angst
build up; the barrios
no longer yawn—they gasp
and the yaws
centuries programmed
burst, spew out
social pus . . .

it can be a rot gut society
when
little wide-eyed children
feel lash and confusion,
fear and retribution,
and
their dreams are
nightmarish glimpses
mimicking dervish deviltry . . .

it is pain,
my son, when your eyes
question
duelos and anxieties,
and you are only four—
how much more
will your tender soul hurt
when you are ten
and
know that life is
dying and death is living?

part of your hurt

is being born Chicano
in
an anglo-ideating culture
that chews up human-ness;
the other part
is being you,
son of my perturbations,
and feeling the anxious
welter that angers me
mirrored in your eyes;
and all we are
confuses you right now
and you adjust
(stifling young soul yearnings),
and
i love you, yet, cannot
keep you from knowledge's
hurting demeanor . . . .

April 30, 1970
AMHERST, MASS.
las flores cantaron
un grito
y la liberación brotó
de un vientre,
welcome
my dear daughter

Libertad was born in primavera

Libertad was born in primavera
como las flores y canciones,
como el amor y lo vital;

dear, sweet child,
little daughter
born, ironically enough,
far from Aztlán
here in Northampton, Massachusetts,
evening of april 29th,
smiling/gurgling,
with your hairy little head
swaying
toward light and sound,
and your exquisite little woman's hands,
delicate and tender,
the fine turning of your curving smile,
and the faint aroma
of freshness
like new grasses billowing
on a new england hillock
when the nip of morn
tucks in spirit,

oh, how sweetly do i love you,
the curious ways your arms stretch out
as if impatient to claim the world
as your own;

yes, you already know
that you have conquered,
for we shall be your doting parents,
and out of love and warmth
delight
in bringing a universe of stars and moons
and silvery thoughts
gliding through the windows of your mind,
and we shall share
warm blankets/pillows/and bedside stories
with milk/cookies
and a smile;
perhaps someday
my hands will spank you,
and the discipline
will not be pleasing,
but you will know, somewhere within,
that love shall weather all;

oh, little delicate being,
with the perfection of your humanity
shining on the ridges
of your stares,
i shall try to understand you
and caress your fears away.
i shall try to be less grouchy,
and at night as you grow older
I shall hold you on my lap,
and together we shall wander
through the furry lands of stories
that will make your heart exclaim;
we shall travel thus together,
you shall sleep upon my lap,
and your mommy's milk shall give you

strength and faith to help you grow;

I shall cry when you are ill,
I shall worry about your safety,
I shall help you stand up strong,
I shall be a helping hand,

    and mi'jita,
    my sweet Libertad-Yvonne,
    we will share with you our love,
    and I hope you get to know
    that in sharing
    truth is needed,
    just like justice/dignity;
    for we've brought you to this world
    through the mystery of birth
and we hope and within want
that you'll grow
into a woman
who'll be free with inner peace,
that you'll never bow nor cringe,
that you'll share in liberty,
ever knowing who you are,
ever proud of where you've come,
that you'll never feel inferior
                    nor superior, Libertad.

may you thus help make life better
for all people of this earth,
that your life will ever mirror
all the meaning of your name . . .

Libertad, sweet child
of bronze skin and glowing eyes,
tender one
with resilience and love
dancing out your smile,
whatever awaits you

we shall ever be there
not just to cuddle you

but to help you weather
storm and to share bounty and joy.

Welcome, mi vidita,
welcome to your home
until someday, years from now,
you will go to create
your own . . . for now this, as ever,
is yours; we don't own you, but
we know the good fortune of being able
to share life with you and you with us.
Libertad, you,
like everyone else,
belong to the world
like the world belongs
to everyone;
share in the process of life
the greatest meaning you can cultivate
from the process of experience;
learn truth and joy,
meaning and dignity,
freedom and peace,
human-ness and compassion,
and forge out of experience
a sense of your own humanity
within the context of our people,
within the context of all people,
that your life
might give comfort when needed
to those who have less,
and that you might know
that to live is to affirm
your awesome human responsibilities
to create, protect, defend, project
the humanity of people,

the sacredness of all life;
take only what is yours by human rights,

share without fear,
trust without hesitation,
love without reason,
but never allow
anything nor anyone to desecrate
the substance of your soul/mind/body.
you are you,
                    not a shadow of your parents,
but you in all your you-ness;
grow to become your best you,
and if you need of us
we shall ever be there,
          for you and Rikárd and anyone,
for love is not to be earned
but neither is it to be toyed with.

love is the poetic feeling
that cries tenderly when i hold you,
it is also strength and dignity,
but never possession.

i love you, mi'jita.

"pack each soul ..."

pack each soul
in love-starred
conundrum
midst the hue, cry, anger
revolution can be,
i, too, am caught
with eyes foraging
for your nearness;

senses merging
becomingonething
you lunge lurchingly
into my arms' hedonism
i caress
the hunger of your lips;

link by link,
we carve a new horizon,
shadows promenade
frenetically seeking
the tautology our union is,
our bodies gesture out
feelings that we are,
our lips affirm the reality we must be;

echo chamber
reverberates our need,
our voices sculpt
our bouyant love & joy,
our hands sort out
our sensate yelp for more,
our minds fill in
anomic yesteryears . . .

new days dawn,
new nights come,
old hurts wander down
and in and out,
around, around we go,
life is a fresh start
wherever we must go;
so dig in now
and let this moment flow,
let senses loose,
implode while i explode—
will love you ever,
no matter where we go—
our lives are one,
though we might be apart,
our lives are one
therein where i reside,
in soul and heart,
in mind and hope and love. . . .

March 10, 1971
otra vez el penco al
estable, back to the calles
y locuras that
hide smirkingly within
e.p.t. twilights,
dreaming mictla dreams

Homing

homing, ese, amidst
old/known faces,
with familia embraces
and love/kisses
flooding each moment
of re-encounter,
la jefita hovering
over her returned children,
carnalas, sobrinos/sobrinas,
suegros, todo el tribu
estrechando bienllegadas;

cruising over to pete duarte's,
chacha marín rapping on the way,
passing familiar sights,
seeing el indio on the streets
walking toward his sense of nirvana,
el hippie flirting with life,
melo curbing on the edge
of his botella,
nina, rosie, rojas, géra,
lupe, lalo, and new faces
within chuco movimiento,
y el borracho
tirando tórica bruta—es algo
rete sabroso being back,
rapping with gardéa, siqueiros,
tony parra, pat,

and host of raza
about building up
mictla publications
to thus change
the horrid imagery
that has ever haunted us;

homing, batos, homing
into the nether world
of causa y sangre y corazón,
and even the caustic words
of lozito (el parole officer)
cannot mar
the happiness
of being back
in this city of callejas y rincones
of pobreza y raza y duelos. . .

homing once again
as i cruise my renault r-10
over the crumbling ruins
of el Diablo, that land of DDT batos
who used to slice up life and hope
with filero and herre,
      shooting up carga/chiva/dreams
into blueridged veins
      hiding beneath la grasa of brown flesh,
finding sanctuary
within the torpor,
                    but life is hell
                    within poverty & self-hate,

homing as i see skeletal remains
of that home that saw me grow
at 3920 Oak, later avenida de las américas,
and now just a dead hulk
where only voices of the past
can find refuge
      if you listen closely—and carnal,

i think even la llorona
used to live in el diablo,
    over by the algodonales del ayer
    there by the river as it cuts/flows
through sand and cactus,
when we used to slip over or under the fence
surrounding Isla de Córdova, that chunk of land
    that méxico used to own, now traded in
as part of the chamizal pact,
and at those ranchitos
where we would trip out on mota/yesca/grifa
and dance
all night
to música rete chicana/mexicana
    y bien rascuache,
or when even younger
we used to slip through the fence
and rip off watermelons, cantaloupes, and chavalas
and the old rancheritos
would threaten us with rusty/dysfunctional shotguns
spraying birdshot
overhead, and we would laugh
with childhood's mirth,
in that barrio del eastside
where i learned
to rub up against willing girls
who wanted to rub up against us

and Doña Chuyita
would run after us,
throwing bricks/rocks—anything she could—
at us and dare us to stop, and we never did,
just shouted at her, and later she would
grab me with her brown/wrinkled tarahumara hands
and between the dark stained bits of teeth
within her 108 year old mouth admonish me
that if she were a few years younger, why,
hell, bato, she would marry me and make
a man out of me, then she would laugh

and tell me to scoot home,
and i would, looking back
at that old/furrowed woman,
india-patarajada from the mountains
of chihuahua
who still chopped wood and ran
through the alleys of my barrio,
barefooted with a red kerchief
tied around her left ankle,
    for strength in running, she would say,
and galavanted about,
Doña Jesusita, Chuyita: Doña Churis,
and we loved her
in our prankster way,
especially when she would sit us down
and regale us with stories
of life in those mountains
when there existed no cars,
just burros and tired people
who knew how to dance and sing
and live off the land;
her face was rivuleted
with time and her eyes
were hawklike and strong,
the folds of skin
on her arms
were skeins of brown earth;
    once she caught me smoking,
    i was fifteen or so, and she
    asked me if my father, Don Pedrito
    approved and I said maybe, puede que sí,
    and i offered her a cigarette,
    she smiled and said that i could not buy
    her silence, that here before the sky
    i would have to know
    that her bosom was not a warehouse
    where secrets could be stored,
but then seeing my youthful fears
    she told me not to worry

for things done in the open are not secrets.
that barrio
now dead and full of shards,
i found a rusty empty can of Mitchell's Beer,
a relic of those times
almost twenty years before
when Mitchell's had reigned
and all the barrio had drunk it,
I found it beside the crumbling wall
of that home my father had painstakingly built
when I had been a four year old toddler,
back then when we had lived
in a one room home
that grew into other rooms
with timely expansions by my father;
i saw remains
of cinderblock fences
where my brothers, Sefy and Pete,
would strum guitars and sing,
and they would tell me
to go inside that it was late,
and in my eight year old world
they seemed big,
for a five and six year span
can mean a totally different world,
and years later
would I come home on leave
to bury them
and cry softly
for the remembrances
culling loneliness in mind/soul;

home again to el paso,
but no longer to my barrio,
but to alien worlds
which had been home for rivals
when I had been tush-hogging
with the X-9 batos,

riding herd on other barrios,
no longer
encaged within the mind searing stench
of Disneyland or the coliseum at rodeo time,
no, seeing
through tears of recollection
a barrio dead, gone into time's shards
with juareños searching through the rubble
for still useful things,
    bricks, boards, iron grill work,
any goddam thing that can be marketed
in los serajeros in south juárez,
    at that enclave of junk yards,
and seeing them take
that still remaining doorframe
from what used to be the doorway to our kitchen
cut my soul
and severed forever
my linkage to my barrio,
and I felt bloody anger
coursing through my mind;

turned, scowling,
to see a superfreeway
being built
to make it easier for tourists
to make it to juárez bistros and whorehouses,
realized
that barrios must make way for progress,
and as i left,
to file another parole report,
heard soft voices of the past. . . .

—virile—

strong, pungent words
cascading, pommeling
burnishing soulmind,
expletive splitting
people complacency,
it plunges deeply . . .

        being permeated,
        it reeks of hell
        midst
        hunger & audacity
        cornucopian dreams
        world flaunting,
        perversity run amuck . . .

virile reality,
life strong and sun-drenched,
life a right, not a privilege,
sacrilege to not live
when we need to explode/implode,
snuffing out mendacity:

        we are not lambs,
        we are not wishes,
        we are not illusions,

        we are the meaning,
        we are the impetus,
        we are the universe . . .

as it courses
through our blood,
and our minds don't genuflect,
the soul resonates
mighty ringing
in our being:

cosmic man,
cosmic reason,
cosmic expletive,

cosmic virility,
cosmic reality,
cosmic virility,
THAT is how
we must exist. . . .

sixth month, twenty-seventh day,
year one thousand, nine hundred
seventy-one
TO SIMON ORTIZ

—vision—

man talked, indian man
proud
of past
when continent was bronze
and buffalo throve,
fruit was good,
chemistry a natural process
 of the universe . . .

i visibly froze thoughts,
 land is not my question,
only the morality of the situation
 involves me . . .

 the land is there
 for those who work it,
 for those whose sweat
   & blood
   & love
   & realness
  have drenched it . . .
i hear my indian brothers,
their questions move me,
and my sanity returns:

 i am more than just a person,
 i reside in nature,
  a bronze flecked man
  caught in the realness of my people . . .

mestizo, son of providence
        merging indio with hispano,
beginning of the cosmic process,
universal man precursor,

that, my brothers, is my vision,
the uniting in love & praxis of all peoples . . . .

sojourning in juarez, poverty
hurts eyes of passersby,
but it hurts those who live
it a hell of a lot more!
10/14/71

we live

we live, die, horribly,
ever unaware
that life must flow
        onward, like heated love
        in twilight hour
        by Santa Fe bridge,
when el paso skyline looms ominous
        against mt. franklin,
        & liquor floods mindsoul,
we feel lost later, almost sunrise,
for the night swam away,
        moment by drunken moment,
        moment by rapid/rabid moment . . .

crossing the bridge, a child slept
        in autumn cold morning nakedness,
        sleep of the dispossessed,
        bare body quasi covered,
        his febrile, hopeful soul quivering;
POVERTY, his, and we were drunk,
        could not realize,
        all that humanity suffers,
        ay, & we are not enough,
        the ultimate question is ever now, yet,
        nothing is enough—it seems—
to un-do the hideous faces   poverty wears . . .

goddamn a world built on perversity,
of money being the predicator,

the sordidness/emptiness
when there is no love
to create societies which care.

that moment is gone now,
       swept into the dust
       of our being drunk in Juárez,
       & the child is dead—probably dead now.
we,   we still live only to someday die
       moment by uneventful moment
       in a world lacking love . . .
ay,   human sadness is a blindness of the soul,
       hurling anger/lust & mania
       onto our paths,
       screeched out words
       leaving gestalt/cathartic murmurs
       on the wind;
we strive to live & become despots
       hovering over others' destinies,
we are a people objectively living, unaware
       that others hurt,
while we are girded by pathological egoism . . . mostly.

—medium point—

medium point
meeting apposition,
     themes written hastily,
justifying
sordid/gruesome projection . . .
     carnal, we cruised streets,
     saw ampleness strut,
     thunders struck me down,
     we drove thunder struck,

     it was dignity
     beatifying
     wintry afternoon,

     later
     we devoured
     celluloided restaurant food,
     still perceiving
     smiling countenance—a
       past promenade
     that awakened animalism—she
       stood buenota

       on my horizon,
     and my loins ached
     and pulsed
       for reclusive haven
       in caverna
       of warmth, love,
     with understanding seeping out
     while i entruncheoned self

        in feminine nirvana;
le vi
tal como ven
ojos that reflect
madness in need
when need is madness,
and she
felt
from afar
my firmament
shaking loose her reservations . . .
        the world continues
        surrounding
        our ravenousness, and we must
        continue maintaining
        semblance of equipoise. . . .

"vi la lluvia anoche, amor mío ..."

vi la lluvia anoche, amor mío,

sentí el duelo
y nos separamos;
hoy te busco
en los callejones
de mi mente/alma

        and i find a shadow
        lurking
        where we last kissed . . .

        sadly, knowingly
        we went our ways
        and still
        memory lingers,
        sticking
to la fibra de mi ser . . .

vi la lluvia anoche, cariño,

te admití
a las avenidas de mi existir;

        you accepted
        and in a lusty, total sense
        love became us . . .

        life is woman,
        but it is more:
        it is mankind loving
        without reason,
        just because love

must exist . . .
it is mankind defending
all and parts . . . it is being aware
we all exist.

from "One Year After: reflections on/about/around the Movimiento. . . ."

NMSU—Las Cruces, NMexico
1/16/1973
NOTE: LIFE IS BACKGROUNDED
BY EXPERIENCE: BY SOUNDS
COMING FROM ONE'S PRIMOR-
DIALITY; BY ALL REALITIES
(factual or imagined!) INTERNAL-
IZED, DEFINED, AND ACTED
UPON: AND BY THE NATURAL
CADENCES OF THE UNIVERSE.
THIS POEM IS ABOUT THOSE
BACKGROUNDING HARMONICS
AND RHYTHMS (tamborazos
are drum beats and gritos are
expletive-kinds-of-self-affirming
shouts—¡Ajúa y cangrejos
y chingazos a los pendejos!).

—Tamborazos y Gritos:
Self Awareness—

phantasmagoria spinning,
mind reeling, soul flaying,

split into infinite senses,
viewing multi-hued idiocies,

providential man
caught in the turbulence of time

when culture becomes

frenetic force and life defines
its own parameters . . .

seed of the universe

sibilantly coursing
its sing-song way,
nurturing its hunger
on soggy piece of land,
fortifying itself to become
        plant, insect, animal, and man,
instinctually seeking out
        a strong foot-hold;

hybrid strength,

never giving in,
from whistling in the wind,
        when currents determined movement
        to that time when buzzing wings
became the growling of the universe,
and still the waiting
for that awesome evolution
when out the swamp and off the trees
would lumber down that sentient being
        whose words and feelings
        a universe of gods and heroes
        would create . . .

man—indigenous man—fearful,
all alone,
viewing the mountains and the swamp,
skimming jungles and desert sands,
man like the granite in the rockies,

man like the cunning of the fox,
man by many names and hues,
        carving out reality
in history's hazy scriptures . . .

                el sol ardiente
                broiled down
                and its cascading rays
                bounced off the rocks,

                    beating cacaphonously
until man with his undulant mind
beat and beat his rhythms on the earth;

tamborazos, tamborazos,
exploding and imploding--

            ca-ta-túm, ca-ta-túm
            ca-túm-ba, ca-ta-túm,

            ma-ca-la-ca, ca-ta-túm,
            ca-túm-ba, ca-ta-túm. . . .

frenetic hands
furiously expounding
hurting/fearful feelings,
and tarahumara, apache, aztec,
zapotec, navajo, pueblo, yaqui,
comanche, chiricahua, y mescalero peoples
searched out the why of life
only to become despoiled
and live a conquered life;

conquered and mestizoed,
once searching hands and minds
became soulful vagabonds
lining up shards of bloody past,
learning español and merging with los amos . . .

new sacrificial peoples,
born to the umbrage of the sun,
molded into the linguistic wishes de
catalán, madrileño, moro,
basque, castellano, judío, y hacendado
plowing off into sun-drenched lands
the sweat cascading down your brow . . .

and the swelling heat
perturbed your sense of quietude

until your lungs expanded,
your soul a grappling/caterwauling need,
y tu garganta cansada,
deadly tired of swallowing your spit,
gritastes aún tu libertad!

¡AAAAAAAAAAYYYYYYYYYYYIIIIIIIIEEEEEEEEE!

aware of brujerías
tus curanderos cure
ills afflicting all realities,
your orators articulate
the need for revolution,
your eyes pierce deep,
scanning through your history,
steeped in la historia,
you now do come awake . . .
            hombre nacido de la selva,
                forjado del maíz,
                mezclado por la vida,
your life and love laments,
cantados por mariachis,
draw histrionic vision
affirming all you feel . . .

y gritas, hombre, gritas
                    ¡AAAAAAAYYYYYYYYYYYIIIIIIIIIIIEEEEEEE!
to the ritmos of tamboras
y lloras, también imploras
la neta de tu vivir . . .

and in between the tamborazos,
in between your atavision,
in between folklorical wishful thinking,
in between your moments of turbulencia,

you now do come awake
with spiritual destitution
growling/howling in your mindsoul.

salvaje/savage in a suit and tie,
flared/bell-bottomed mentality
freewaying your reality
into insipid grifa trips,
seeking aztlán in every destitute puff,
your eyes redden
with soggy thoughts,
revolucionario de conveniencia,
raving
        ranting
often panting,
searching for a lost quivira
amidst amerikan plasticity . . .

goaded by ego-mania,
girded by marihuana,
bato de la nueva ola,

   DON QUEJOTO TAN MANCHADO,
your windmills are institutions
which cast you afloat from yourself.

hijos del sol,
sons of pyramid builders,
progeny of gitanos,
artesans of lost arts,
weepers in welfare lines,
collectors of movements and buttons,
surveyors of new resolve,
      ay, we, yes we,
          who shelter our reality
          in taco bells and howard johnsons
          and conspire to foment
          38 different flavors of cultural revolutions

        paid for with master charge &
          american express,
        who ply our craft skilfully
        through O.E.O., H.E.W., H.U.D., & IDIOCY
        who bargain out our lives
        in every market place
        and feel ashamed
        to even now proclaim
        that we, as man, have come
        on a journey from the earth,
    crawled out of rock and swamp,
    conjointed by the sun
    to live and love and be
    a testament to truth,
    a testament to life,
    a puff of earth and time . . .

and we are earth
with its cutting rivers flowing,
its billowing clouds
creating cragged mountains
on sibilant wind trajectories,
sentient feelings
lonelily acknowledging
deracination,
        hurt/confused
        hoping/needing,

      and the world we somehow survive
      burns its frigid rigidity into us,
      our souls cauterize
      and our minds accept
      criss-crossed calloused patterns,

and in our drunken moments
we forget to be un-real,
our past(s) zoom(s) in,
we hear tamboras interspersed

with frenzy and guitarras,
and we cry out the anguish of the moment,
we dance and sing,
we shout and celebrate,

we weep and groan
        desirous of explosion,
we face our lives
        as we prepare to die,
we live, we live,
        aún así gritamos
                ¡AAAAAAAAAAAYYYYYYYYYYYIIIIIIIIIIIEEEEEEEEE!

we live, we live
for momentary sketches,
afraid, afraid

to face up to our being(s),
we cringe and hope
that we shall last forever,
forgetting thus
our being made of earth. . . .

—fui, soy, seré—

liberation,
like the wind,
caresses the soul
& ruffles the mind . . .
Born unto the sun, drenched by its madness, burnt . . .
vagabond mind, meandering soul, pallbearer for the universe.

. . . no lloro por liberación,
pues cantogrito liberación.

como los peñascos
existo en el universo,
hombre hecho del hierro,
    curtido como el trigo y maíz,
            cast into a mestizo mold
en las montañas me miro
como piedra:
        granite strength
        unafraid to assail
        wind, water, and time . . .
i am time, time spent tubularly, round slick time . . .
funneling my unsanity, mod dressed quixote sitting by
windows, the world on edge of thoughtfeelings, multitudes
stream by . . . being-ness peopled by thought & lack of
thought; some minds without frontiers
pícaramente

rivulet their undulant capriciousness in and out of our
lives feeling that there exists no meaning to being—others
cling to static needs—
        cling, cling, CLING

dragging mendacity out their souls,
hiding demons forcing them on . . .

Who was i before the shaping of my face? Crocodile ooze in
swamp, leery of stepping out to sprout out wing and claw?

germinal seed
enmeshed within the soil,
ensnarled by its warmth
nurtured by water and vapor,
radiated by the sun . . .

i was all and nothing,
coming from el "nadaísmo,"
circuitous fabric of la vida
frothing fearful creature, founder of universality, the
genesis of thought—definer of the world . . .
todo existe
en la mentealma,
la mentealma es
elusive, amórfica—
las ideas no tienen cuerpo
y todo es nada . . .
but even dust has body, texture . . . but ideas? ay, who am
i now that my face is molding itself? Fearful nose that
doesn't want to smell what all i am! Deodorized and
sanitized, sanforized and scrutinized!

man sprouting many colors,
mind rebelling against itself,
hands caressing all they kill,
wanton soul defiling nature . . .

but i am more—an infinity of more-ness! i am human
pandemonium, tragic figure comically encapsulating flux of
life . . . silver winged bird, a technological trajectory,
creator of plasticity . . . cool & salient mind

prescribing for the universe

the loss of all that's visceral,
from all i'll take the blood,
from all i'll take the passion,
from all i'll take the hurt . . .

yet—oh, damn, but true—i still am more . . . i am the
resonance of time, that anguish of starvation, that void that
cries for love . . . and i am love

love that thrives in madness,
gitano love of contradicting life,
amor que en alma vive,
sonrisas que dan luz . . .

Who shall i be after the shaping of my face? Mindsoul
knowing no barriers, existential paradox creating new
awareness!

mountain, river and cloud,
buildings, bridges and systems,

i shall be nadaísmo, rivulet of time,
i shall be todoísmo, sliver of space,
space undifferentiated,
hypnotic smoke wafting,

undulant hope and trust,
galvanizing catalyst,
majestic human being,
fearful/tragic human life,

two hands able to caress
your many existent realities,

knowing no fears of you
soul laminated by the rainbow . . .

fui/soy/seré
time bound, duty stretched,
mortal and unaware,

my horizons drill into my eyes,
my reality flails my hope,
but love is the foundation
that girds
my seeing each new being
as worthy of being loved.

More than

more than being horny,
i merely affirm
a reality of certainty
                    as my loins ache/seek
sexuous/serious
encounter(s)
with damn-right/godly woman,

one able to sustain
my furious sense
                    of being
            macho able to love
tenderly, fully & unreservedly
woman/women
who strongly affirm(s)
awesomely stirring/beautiful humanity,
            not just breast size
nor slick-mag smile
nor smart-tight-fanny clothes/wiggle,
but spirit/mind encased
within sensitive body
willing to share
magic of blood sensation in veins
with moving/touching/kissing/caressing
so that movement can be entered
and explosion/implosion
can signal more than one
transport
to where one feels
imagery and meaning . . .

not out of need
nor fear to be alone,
but out of awareness/appreciation
do loins/soul pulse
in rhythm
with mind
within the universe of love shared
as another linking moment
in time's continuum
is caressed.

come let sunlight
see us be
communion
within the space
of now's sensuality.

May 28, 1973
Steven's Point, WIsc.
in green &
mechanized lands
thought ripens slowly

Siendo / *being*

siendo	being
un momento	a moment
perdido en sueño,	dream-lost,
creyendo	believing
todos idiotismos,	all idiocies,
flotando en alma	soulfully floating
como llanto espantoso	within your breast
en tu ceno, mujer	like a lament, woman
que engordas	who fattens
mi percepción	my perception
es fácil querer	it is easy
tu realidad	to love your reality
cuando perdido estoy	when lost am I
en tu mirada—	within your fantasy—
todo dentro	everything within
lo oscuro	obscurity
se ve	is seen
como sentimiento,	like sentient feeling,
hasta que	until
se reconoce el vivir. . . .	living, itself is realized. . . .

cronchis   cronchis   cronchis   cronchis   cronchis   cronchis

translation by Sánchez

En lo frágil

en lo frágil de un pétalo,
    my son,
I visualized you
before I knew you—
it was, mi'jo, back then
in my own youth,
you were the swelling
in Teresa's womb,
kicking, wanting
air to burst
through the fragile petal
a loving womb is . . .

nine years ago,
you were born to feel loving arms and energy,
I then was just awaiting
knowing you, yet,
I first had to be away
four years,
        entombed in texas prisons,
and I really met you
when you first embraced
a prodigal father just returned
with a stripe seared mind,
and through your loving being
I was resurrected
and once again alive . . .

gracias, mi'jo, gracias
for the normalcy
you've given me.

Teresa, last night

Teresa, last night
we drank, danced
y gritamos
as mariachis sang
joyous songs;

      the músicos
      serenaded us,
      love songs
         that moved our spirits
      years ago
      when in our need to know
      each other's life
      we clung
         to fragile moments
      and saw new worlds beckoning
      in our words;

years later,
    a prison sentence
and four-year separation and
two children later,
we've once more
sought out ternura y cariño,
expressing them again
within
the worlds—of música, palabras,
and searching hands/lips/realities—
we lovingly create & re-create
within the delicate balance
        of our separate realities
        as we coincide through time/space

and mutually give shape
to naturaleza in its universal sense
          of duality as it creates oneness of life;

having refound you
so many times,
in moods, moments, caresses, and sharing,
reconozco que solamente
     te quiero,
tal como quiero/aprecio
     el poder vivir,
          vibrantemente. . . .

Mi'ja

mi'ja, child clutching on,
smiling,
          hopeful niña,
with three year old hopefulness,
singing your innocent joys;

tus ojitos llenos
de estrellitas danzantes,

you revel in benedictively being
          aware
that your family loves you
beyond the moment,
beyond furtive hopes
     and shadowy fears,
so you playfully
pull my beard,
          mimic mama, and
squealingly
act out your needs,
          mi'ja, mi Libertad . . .

January 14, 1974–2 a.m.
En mi cantón
El Pasiente, Tejas
Momento de la Garrapata
gris/nocturna . . .

"Liberation begins . . ."

Liberation begins in the mind/soul and is legitimized by meaningful and direct action. It is nurtured by the love and appreciation we have for ourselves and others. It is the wellspring from which comes purpose in life. There ultimately exists the choice: liberation or enslavement. In a world of vertical mobility, bosses, masters, and oppressors, there exist only dehumanization and oppression. To define others as lower or higher is to resign oneself to being a digit, an object, a slave—for there must then exist a scale that will determine our worth, just like any object in any store. To define all people as human and meaningful is to assure that one is worthy as all people are worthy and that one shall defend one's humanity from oppression and share in the human struggle in mutual concert with others to help create a diverse and humane universal social order for all to participate in. To exploit the environment and other people is to act wantonly and inhumanly—for the world's riches belong in equal portion to all human beings, not just to the swift and conniving, but to all. Our individual worth shall come from our self definition as long as it is in harmony with a universal dignity, worthiness, and justice. Peace shall be the offspring of liberation.

from "On Being: Hacia la liberación popular"

February 20, 1974
11:30 a.m.
El Paso Airport
AA Flight 116 to Chicago
death is more
than one dimension,
this mood is two,
one personal
and the other general;
one is Hallack
and the way he lived
within thought,
the other
is death touching all.

". . . Come lovely and soothing death,
Undulate round the world, serenely arriving, arriving,
In the day, in the night, to all, to each,
Sooner or later delicate death . . ."
          —Walt Whitman, *Leaves of Grass*

To/for Hallack McCord, Denver friend, Death, be not soft

Friend, comrade, brother,
bearded wise one
seeing beyond illusions,
reading people's realities

on the sinewy lines
of the back of the left hand—

      Death, be not soft,
      be affirmative, visceral,
      as life has been . . .

you accosted the hues
of Sonoma II's wishy washiness
with laughter and love;

        Be as the turbulence
        of spring growling
        its new sprung hungers
        to imprint its visage
        on time's continuum . . .

Your lionish mane,
reddened by many years,
flew in that Northern
California clime
as you chucklingly
acknowledged time
socializing the fearful;

        Be as burnishing
        as summer quietude's
        chemistry remaking
        earth's springy verdure
        into waves of grass
        undulating
        in the wind . . .

Hallack, Denver friend
who hypnotized
a menagerie of doctoral aspirants,
the whimsy of life and death
danced through the fabric
of your humanity;

        Be as surfeited
        as fall billowing
        in yellows/oranges/
        and burnished browns,
        the beginning of
        creaking tiredness . . .

and though a stroke/coma
have claimed your body,
and though the very earth
is now your umbrage,
I, like others touched by you,
recall that salient figure
reading on a Sonoma dude ranch porch
and undulating/wafting
through our minds,
you smiled often
with a mature, caring assuredness
and ensnared
a spirituality
that was unassailable . . .

       Be as wise as winter,
       cloaked in snowy shroud,
       aged umbrage for the spirit,
       aglow in awareness
       that to live is also
       to someday die . . .

Hallack, this morning
John Pool called
from the Denver airport;
    "I have bad news, Ricardo,"
he feelingly said,
    "Hallack never came out
    of his coma—he passed away . . ."
my hurry in packing
to go to Urbana
became snarled
by memories
of moments spent
in jive and banter
by a California poolside,
when dialectics of social survival
skimmed off mind's edge;

you shared much, Denver old friend,
and we laughed
at all our foibles,
then at that old café
for sunday breakfast
and later
when your experienced life
balked at societal exaggerations,
and you spoke at different times
of multifaceted survival
as a human being; you lived/cared . . .

        Death, whitmanesque danze
        gazing/promenading
        into the infinite finiteness
        of our human lives,
        sorting out of reason
        to sift us through
        your myriad ways,
        taking each unto eternity,
        where the soul can reflect
        on its once
        human travails;
        equalizer/fortifier,
        some only survive,
        others live creatively,
        yet everyone
        must you embrace
        to thus affirm
        their having been
        more than a transient hope . . .

Hallack,
you created
your imprint
upon time/space,
and became indelible
in the poetic way

you shared
el proceso de la vida . . .

    Death, be not soft,
    be a song affirming
    that what has been
    was good, and that
    which shall be
    shall be fruition
    of humane ideals . . .

au revoir, Denver old friend, au revoir.

Smile floating

smile floating
through fringe of thought,
adulterous hopes/dreams
built
on the silk
of her lips
skimming mind's eyes visage

        she is beautiful
           like most women are,
        and i rigidify
           tautological manhood
        tripping
           of caressing
        nyloned thighs
           and silkened fanny,
and dream is broken
by rasping voice
announcing
      NORTH CENTRAL FLIGHT 985
        to Lansing

and i trudge on
toward other trips. . . .

April 18, 1974
Denver airport
waiting for flight to el paso,
3 1/2 hour layover, walk,
look at magazine rack,
have some coffee,
walk some more/
see the people,
walk, Ricardo, walk,
see me walk, jeez,
but i feel like a
refugee from zavala
elementary; someone once
told me that weirdoes
are as common as
chinaberry trees . . .
i realize that i
exist in my own world
as others
exist in theirs . . .

3rd world umbrage

not to seem lost,
but being afloat in airports
dizzies one;

the corridors ferment
with buzzing of lonely voices
seeking information;

used to be
that 3rd worlders
did not fill up corridors
in airport lounge areas,
just cleaned them,
now we do both,
and in killing time
i notice

the umbrage of the 3rd world,
its strong women
who are realizing their right
to dignity
and no longer need dye hair
nor get it straight
nor assume
gloria steinem posture,
for Chicanas can struggle
for liberation as Chicanas
and not as emulators
            of media chic,
and so can Black/Native & Asian American
women . . .

umbrage of the 3rd world,
the sense of life
that woman—black,
                    chicana, puertorican,
                latina,
            asian,
                    native american—
can give
to mind/soul/body;
real visceral women
who
smile in strength/joy,
walk musicatingly,
love passionately,
and articulate
    the many worlds
            they inhabit
with the sensitivity
that struggle gave them . . .

black women
who bask majestically
as they realize

that being real comes
from life's ferventness
as they assert
that black is beautiful;

latinas who
regale the environment
with a heritage
of love/understanding
and affirm nuances of being
from chicana to borícua
to argentina,
peruana and all
the senses of being
they have existentially experienced;

native american women,
sylvan/joyous,
real and visceral
like ideas
expressing
the sensual naturalness
of the universe & people;

asian women
who configurate all realities
into life's essence
and caress
the breeze
that beautifies the earth;

sensitive, alert, intelligent, beautiful, total women
who make each moment of life
a palatable experience
in the sharing process of love . . .
    to live is to love/share
        within the context of people/earth.

En la sangre

en la sangre
del barrio
leading to dropping out
del escuelín
only to die
nine years' worth
in soledad and la tejana,
horrid prisons
striping on racism,
lo vital became
the movimiento of the '60s
when prison doors
released body,
and la causa
burned
its bronze locura
onto mind/soul

marchas, sangre y chingazos,
and people like lalo,
tijerina, chávez, tigre pérez,
and others proffered up
hope
   and
      corazón,

                      it changed a bit,
pero los balazos y la jura
                      still persist,
y las calles
todavía tienen fríos,
y los desmadrazgos
                      still permeate

los barrios
que habito,
pero ahora reconozco
          that to struggle is to be,
          and to be is
          to struggle
          toward liberation,
          for in that process
          is human-ness affirmed. . . .

May 10, 1974
trío de locos
in juárez bistros,
drinking/listening
to mariachis . . .

Fridays belong to friends, sometimes

fridays belong to friends, sometimes,
when Horacio "Chacho" Minjarez,
Rafa "Chafa" Aguirre, and I
can galavant all night
from cantina to cantina,
jiving with the pimps
as they shout out:
      "Say, can you spare a messican minute, fellows,
      and i'll take you to see the girls,"

and his mouth opens in surprise
as one of us shouts back jivingly,
      "No, ese, we want to see the boys,
      damn the girls,"
and we walk/saunter laughingly
up different streets,
stopping
with don cojón-chon,
buy little french rolls,
      sliced in half and stuffed
      with avocado, mexican cheese,
      jalapeños, and a dash of salt,
and we continue
in our camaraderie
walking up juárez avenue
to carlos or the manhattan or the san luís
to hear mariachis and shout,
all the time eating tortas,

winking at the women,
alluding to ourselves
as being non-tourists
in this city on the border;

we enter the manhattan,
and mariachis serenade us,
and the tourist trade is thick,
aguirre squirms and says
let's go to another place
as young horacio bolts about,
splashing his tequila doble on his shirt,

and we walk down and cross the tracks,
get in the car and drive
across that stretch
of supertourist traps;

swarming streets
filled with hungers of amérika,
seekers of sexual bliss,
we laugh,
for we just came to drink
and shout and pay mariachis
for their art . . .
we enter the San Francisco Bar,
expecting music to blare out,
we drink and wait for them,
and then realize
that May 10th
is always
Mexican Mother's Day,
and good mariachis
make more money
          serenading
home to home
than in bars,
and these mariachis are the best,
so they'll play

out on the streets,
and we mope and start to talk;

Chacho is a youth
who wants to write
and film
and live
a legendary life
while creating sketches
of reality
on the canvas of our souls,
he is a poet,
            young and strong,
and full of vision,
and he reminds me
of garcía lorca and whitman
and rimbaud
and baudelaire
and lalo
and salinas
and more especially of himself,
and his quick mind
pounces on every word;
all night long rafa and i revel
in the magic
of the word worlds Chacho gives us,
he wants to go to yale
to whip it,
and he will,
and rafa is moved to tears
by Chacho's words,
and i feel strong/good
in meeting such a delicate/virile/affirmative mind/soul
as this young bato
who speaks of years at jefferson high
and the projects and the fact that he and his mother
survive somehow on about $1000, yes one thousand dollars,
a year,
yet, he believes in himself, in raza, in the struggle

and
we sense him puffing out his chest,
he's gonna tell us something,
aguirre in his forty years of life
has learned patience
and he listens,
and i, in 33, have learned
how to bob/weave/and jive,
so i jive,
and we three laugh,
rap on
til we tire
of the blandness

of music-less bars,
and walk out into the street,
and as we rave and jive and galavant
we hear the far off strains
of inebriated music makers,
over there
in that club on the corner,
yes, tontos, there,
sí, at the forum,
we enter, sit, order
bohemias for rafa and me,
a tequila doble for horacio
he's beginning to get high,
      "I really don't drink, I, ah er. . ."
we let it go at that and smile,
mariachis come on over,
toquen, we say,
we say,
something
for our friend here (Chacho),
it's mother's day, and for his age
he's a hell of a mothuh, he is,
so it's his day,
now play "Las Mañanitas,"

or something to that effect,
we laugh and jive,

and $23 later
we walk out of that joint,
drive over to max-fim's
and look at ballroom waltzers,
and drink a round or two and
drive back to el paso. . . .

polygenetic man, Ack,
you merge well
with humanity . . .

—Ack—

Ackley, friend,
  mongol,

    ukrainian,
    angloized teacher
    within Lumbee Indian construct . . .

ackley, young/old man
grappling with your people,
        those white racists,
you growl, expect change,
        they cringe . . .

it destroys you
little by little,
man with penchant
        for sotol, mescal, tequila, y ron,
you swim
in your world's perversity . . .

you, ackley,
are not malicious,
you, victim of your people's history,
weep out
guilts of indio/chicano reality,
you've shared and shown that you give a damn,
it's not your fault, it's theirs.

you reach out embracingly,
        feel hurt/anomic
        when put down

it is not a put-down,
just our reality . . .
we like you,
that's why we jive
in our own manner with you. . . .

Pedro-Cuauhtémoc Sánchez
born January 16th, 1975
died January 31st, 1975

—Sonriente Duelo—

escarcha doliente,
tu sonrisa
strained through plexiglass; tubes, wires, and machinery. . .
your heart's rhythm galvanizing feeling . . .
Sí, niño
you had but one day to live, to survive since that day you
were born, and you refused to listen to medical opinion, so
you fought bravely
como tu sangre encomendaba
and you survived just over fifteen days, living in that glass
cage, breathing artificial air, gurgling with fury and hope
for your right to also walk this earth . . . we had no money
to fly in superspecialists, for Boston's cardiological
masters must need money to make such trips . . . so we did
only what we could, fighting right beside you for all that
we could muster . . .
HIJITO, ay, pero mi
Pedrito-Cuauhtémoc, you who would be someone to share life
with, tan grande que te mirabas,
tus manitas bien formadas
y tu cuerpo tan lleno,
como si ya estuvieras listo
para embarcarte en plena lucha social
but no! ya estavas
en la lucha mayor,
in that awesome struggle within the
claroscuro/dentro la tiniebla/
between life and death, and you waged your mighty battle,
m'ijo, y cuando nos dijeron

83

that you had just died, we hurried back to hold you with
love, hurt, and pride, pride that for a couple of torrid
weeks a warrior had visited our humble beings and taught us
that to live is but to struggle toward the conquest of our
fears. . .
you smiled much, hijito,
y lloramos todavía
pero andamos
en el conocimiento
que la muerte no es extraña,
it is part and parcel
del proceso vital . . .

      Pedrito-Cuauhtémoc, m'ijo
como flor aborning in time's filament,
      pedazo de amor
caught in timorous fragility
      twixt life and death,
surviving but 15 days,
      you visited us briefly
in those days of hopeseared pain
      and imprinted
your life's beauty on our mindsouls . . .
      we love you
within
      and beyond
the spaces you made yours, m'ijo . . .

tierra y ceniza
y esperanza en la brisa,
i recall you beyond your lifespan,
i recall you aunque
la mente dice adiós, cariño,
adiós, hijito querido,
te recuerdo siempre
en tu vibrante vitalidad
y lucha
con tu sonrisa bella
enconejada . . .

"should i look for you ..."

should i look for you
in hopes
drenched by fears?

how can hands and lips
caress your reality,
if
you
continuously hide it
within diaphanous fears?

how can i celebrate
your vital forces
if
you
cloak them
with societal configurations?

how can meaning
be shared
when
it is shrouded
by childhood's miasmically montaged mandates
and camouflaged
by grandiloquent
circumnavigations?

in Boulder, Colorado, in may of '74
six brothers/sisters met death
in two cars exploded by dynamite
two days apart... now a year later,
we've met to commemorate... ay,
let cantogritos pierce the air...
Boulder, may 26, 1975

—se dejarán—

se dejarán en el tiempoespacio
sus sangrientas huellas
writing
on history
the horrid reality
of our fears and desperation . . .

carnalas/carnales,
ardiente gente,
it is recorded
in the way you lived
that death
would somehow stamp
reality on your fates . . .
ay, caray,
you becried
imperialismo
and vaulted your beings
into a horrendous struggle
wherein the enemy would merge
its many colored faces
into the grotesquerie
of the unknown . . .

ay, canto a Neva,
canto a Florencio,
canto a Una,
canto a Francisco,

canto a Reyes,
canto a Heriberto,

y hoy con Antonio, the survivor,
gritamos
hacia una liberación
enbarcándonos
a ese coyuntamiento
wherein
we can realize
that the struggle
must be shared
in dignity, love, & self-defense . . .

ay, canto neta
which rings
in the mindsoul,
stirring
our whirring social insanity,
strung in the ritmos
of blood,
      ay blood of our people
      in the struggle,
cry of desesperación
in the heat
of all oppression,
we must do more
than hope or cringe or pray,
tenemos que organizarnos
      y prepararnos,
that being alive
might become
una celebración vital,
that we might realize
that bowing & begging
are not the way to live . . .

let this blood-soaked earth,
caked with all oppression,
re-awaken
to our heated need
for liberation,
let today

become a beacon
to our thinking,
        that feelings might jell
and that
we might
this nation condemn
for the hunger, destitution,
        and all the other ills
        genocidally destroying
        our juventud . . .

there is no moment
to commemorate,
nor a bicentennial
to celebrate,
hay nomás
la aclaración
que el vivir
        debe ser libre,
cada momento lleno,
y eso implica
una batalla
        to recoup
all that has been stripped from us . . .

let our streets awaken
to a feeling of our being
SOVEREIGN HUMAN BEINGS,
Raza que va vivir
at whatever the cost;
let us be aware

that we must plan
our liberation
and thus unite
to fight our common fight,
coyuntándonos al fin,
alive
in the strength and beauty
of our vitalismo . . .
ay, gente,
tenemos que obrar/labrar,
our minds fortalized by meaning
        and our souls pulsing con ritmos
del aprecio vital,
stating with our very beings
that if life is to have dignity,
we must, al fin, declare
ourselves
inviolate, ready, willing
        to create
obras de liberación . . .

gente, let not tears of despair
        nor empty hopes
        desecrate
the memory of those fallen
in the struggle,
let us rather realize
that today
we march
in solidarity,
seeking to know each other
and ourselves
in order
to declare
that we shall liberate
our lives,
and in that way
pay loving homage/tribute to

those who in the struggle died . . .
    ay, canto a Neva,
        canto a Florencio,
        canto a Una,
        canto a Francisco,
        canto a Reyes,
        canto a Heriberto,
    y abrazo antonio. . . .

hacia la liberación popular
y vámonos recio, raza.

"raza mindsouls . . ."

raza mindsouls
breaking down
walls, bars,
and racist
misconceptions,
realizing
that each one
of us can dare
create,
can dare defend
the destiny
we'll all build—
al fin seremos libres
but only if we struggle
with all that we can be:
   our minds, our souls,
      our beings
in raza harmony.

from "Tinieblas Pintas Quebradas"—
"Shattered Prison Darknessess"

—POEM: love sensation—

feeling surging, splurging—
a canticle emanating,
the soul cauterizing, the mind congealing—
breath fulminating,
      heated, passionate,
you paint hurt within,
      become mindsoul's portraiture,
you roseate worlds,
      fomenting strong eviscerations,
you fragment universes
      deracinating sanity . . .

mind's mirror, soul's mirage,
total being, a cosmic collage . . .

      burning, churning,
      volcanic reality,
      molten like my innards . . .

you, poem, a love sensation,
immersed in my being,
awesome phantom
haunting inner solitude,
creation of my loins
hectically longing,
          ay, somewhere i languish . . .

wispy caterwauling demons
careening in my soul,
yet,
soft allure, tender reflection
gestating in soul's gut lining;

song, spasmodic, melodic, sonorous,
flinched out,

paradoxical joy/lament,
liberation is double thighed,
                    a fire-strewn acclamation,
indulgence and negation,
reality of being,
flirtation with totality . . .

being—a poem
          burnt
          onto the pages
          of a life lived fully!

prisons, barrios, &
universities later,
the sky is soup y
la quemaduría suele
ensecar the naiveté
de lo jovenazo pasado . . .

L. Chukosburgo, Te(de)jaslum
5 de noviembre, 1976
conatl/sapoteotls

—in soup of timespace:
sorts—

gelatina y garras
entre miserias y sonrisas
brisas
curten
tiempoespacio
con saludos helados y huecos,

they glide about,
sensing life
and cast about their shells,
hucksters
hustle
tired people, hope is their ploy,
born again vagabonds
whip up jívaro jive

viviremos, compiras, beyond
the tenuousness
brought about
by artless gawkers
asking
silly readers' digest
undigestible questions

    "say, bro, how long

did it take to write
that pome
or to slap paint
in mural form
upon that seedy looking wall?"

it took
huevos and hambre and desmadre
and a few renegaded thumbs down at dios, bro,
and then it took more hurt
and begging and a whole pot-full
of restless nights and damnable days . . .

so the art continues churning/burning,
until
it all comes out:

love, caresses, and need
cascading down on realization,
and it becomes
a hodgepodge book
laughing
its diabetic madness
while estocazos verdugos
esculpen
realidades calurosas
entre montañas de vientres,

manos, labios, dedos,
and other salubrious extremities
celebrate
pedacitos de amor,

and hurting/impotent people
line up at revco drugstores
to purchase
medicare packages of cochatín,
vergamicina, and panocharín,

caldío casi frío
y mermelada cast in cantogritos

wobbly sensations
from soledad to huntsville tejas joint
to yale unto P(oeta) h(ighly) D(emented),
pedagogical ex-con, los invito
with put-on frivolity
to a world
frothing at its margins
with monstrous imagery
and priestly primordial screams,

espacio curtido por tiempo
    en su caldío,
sueño lujosas mujeres
    bebiéndome
mientras vivo picardías
    lloviéndome,

y entre las pelusas noches
i scheme on nuns y otras
    attached & unattached women
while plotting mostly unworkable plots
against any and all systems . . .
there exists little daylight
within my nocturnally primal scream,

just minute shafts of light
burrowing into the feralness

de mi mentealmacuerpo . . .
    thus . . .
i write and write and write and writhe. . . .

ironies abound, still
life must be lived . . .
Chukesville, Te(de)jaslum
6 de Nov. 1976 conatl/sapoteotls

—y después de—

y después de años,
many years later,
with a doctorate
sigo andando las calles
de mi pueblo
walk into employment agency,
later to texas welfare department
seeking foodstamps,
young welfare worker
fills out forms
then sees me as a person,
stutters out
a stammered
      "Hm, Ricardo Sánchez, Ph.D.,
      are you the . . . the . . . the . . . ?"

i answer
a mere yes,
meaning
i could be the
whatever
you might think i be,
inside smiling, one
of those don't give a damn smiles,
and await . . .
      "You aren't here to gather material
      to write an exposé, are you?" he asks.

no, just for foodstamps,
pues estoy quebrado
   y jodido,

my kids must eat, you know,
and my entrails shake and quiver,
feel both suicidal & homicidal,
sanity is a thin line, it wiggles
and i could fall any moment
if i don't think . . . am back to 1965
reactions
when my first born was about to be
and in desperate fear i robbed,
now a similar yet distinct feeling
burns through,
the doctorate was for naught, so
were the writings, but have to hurl out
words and thoughts, must write,
and somehow go beyond a tenuous survival.
no longer hate, just want to create
beautiful worlds to share with all,
just want to live. . . .

within
it growls,
sometimes it sings,
it courses its way
and creates its own beauty . . .
EPT Dec., 1976

we are a people quite integral

we are a people quite integral in being; it is our nature to
take pride in what we are—and though experience can hurt and
also cripple, we have survived and in so doing have created

a sense of being-ness
which flavors
our speech patterns,

we sing—
we dance—
we shout
to all our poetry,
our art reflects
the fusing of our languages,
we feel alive
whichever way we speak,
our words are thesis,
antithesis,
& synthesis,

we spiral forward
within our upward movement,
as we create
from praxis
a new language,

one that is vibrant, alive, and filled with pensive
strength.

from "Thoughts on Language"

within
it growls,
sometimes it sings,
it courses its way
and creates its own beauty . . .
EPT Dec., 1976

flow on, palabras

flow on, palabras parpadiadas, como llantos
iluminando
paisajes,
somos hechizos
linguísticos
derrotando mundos secos
y estructurando universos
        de policolores,
somos sueños muy chicanos
curtiendo los dones castellanos
y netamente distorcionando los ingleses,

nos enloquecemos
cuando nuestras panoramas
nos cubren estéticamente
y desarrollamos
principios fundamentales

de la cumbre humanizante,
somos una raza cósmica
cristalizando
un universo bronceado,

and why should we almost apoplectically apologize for being such as we are, a
people who have merged bloods, cultures, languages, and facets of historicity into
an intricate, complex, and very balanced existentiality? . . . We are an integral people
whose sense of being is one of fusion, and in that fusing process we have taken ele-
ments of both worlds in order to create a tertiary perspective—an interlinguality—
that creates different and newer nuances of valuation for being-ness.

from "Thoughts on Language"

"so we must love ..."

so we must love,
love
beyond all reason,
     love without a reservation,
         love without expecting a return,

we m.ust embrace
all living things . . .

         unshackled in mindsoulbody
         prepared to share
         or to defend
         whatever is defensible,
         beyond contrivance,
         realistically, . . .

no prissy words nor honeyed deeds,
beyond objectified intentions,
we'll meet as complete children, women, men,
         yes, más allá of the conflicts,
         we'll dialogue,

it will all depend
if we've the courage
to remember
the sordid ways
     we've hurt each other,
if we've the courage and the strength
to right our many wrongs—
         for if we do,
         we'll then be able to create

a humanizing social schema
and we'll live freer—

        beyond our wildest dreams. . . .

from "Más Allá of the Conflicts"

—quiero a la poesía—

quiero a la poesía
como quiero la sangre
latiendo en mi ser,
i feel it, think it,
realize it, fight it,
and accept its consequences,
just as i accept the many functions
      of my being
      a man with mindbodysoul,

ay, poetry cries, shouts, sings,
laments, wails, and connives,
it simply exists
like mountains, clouds, and wind,
it is sound
when a child gurgles or cries,
or the rich, full curves of a loved woman,
it is furrowed earth
      or the wrinkled reality
      of a complete person
      who has lived fully,

ageless,
poetry is release and affirmation,
the consummation of a relationship,
ay, it warbles and bleeds,
      caresses and slaps,
es la ética of our integrity,
an aesthetic confirmation
of our humanity . . .

poetry
    is
      what
          i
        offer
            you
              in
          ensuing pages, a glimpse
              of mine mindsoul . . .

a thousand thoughts & feelings
careen, it is late night,
where is up from here? everywhere!
el paso, texas, el cantón
dec. 12, 1976

—y from here, where?—

y from here, where?
it might appear
in moments of frustration
a bleak future,
but i live,
my family lives,
and many friends exist,
multi-hued friends
who reach out & share,
who love without demanding
   anything in return,
their being warm, tender,
and supportive
becomes a cornerstone for me,
and
even though
there are those
   who strive only to hustle me,
the real people
who partake of life with me & mine
make it possible
to see beauty
in the awesomeness of being . . .

from here to wherever
i shall go
to thrive and live and celebrate,
striving to ever dialogue,
to also see the bitter and the joyous,
for the life process

is one wherein we truthfully acknowledge
 the things that please
and those that cause us pain,
i realize that i shall die,
thus i want to live all the more
until my death arrives,
that there might never again
exist
regrets of having failed
to live . . .

there is a glorious world
that rainbows always paint,
            its colors run the gamut
            from bronze to black to white,
and in between are reds & yellows,
& all their mergings also,
y yo, un ser humano,
afirmo lo que soy,
and say
            that all the world I'll know,
and in my knowing it,
I'll learn to love
            its differences,
and in my loving it
I'll learn to love
            my people,
for life revolves around us,
while we revolve también;

del mundo yo nací
para vivir en él,
y ahora reconozco
que nunca olvidaré
las sangres que yo cargo
ni el nombre que me dieron,
for in such strength I'll live;
aware of who I am,
I now can journey forth

to meet with anyone
and in our meeting say,
      you're human just as I,
      and though our cultures differ,
      we both do have a right
      to live as humans should,
        with dignity and justice,
        as peaceful people should;

I realize my duty
calls first for love and meaning,
but those can only come
when one defends
one's being
and that of family/friends;
there can be no forgetting
the rights that one is born with;
      to humanize oneself
      is to affirm one's being
      and to affirm one's being
      is simply to confirm
        the people that one springs from
        as being worthy of
          the love that one can muster
          in a creative process
          that sings out WE ARE ONE;
if one of life is worthy,
all people must be so,
but one must realize
that some mistake our loving
      for being but a weakness
        and if they try to harm us,
        we MUST defend our lives,
      so let us then join hands
      with all who are oppressed,
      and with our joining say
        we all are one in nature,
        and for freedom thus we fight:

we'll fight that you might be
whatever you so wish,
we'll fight that women be
as dignified as possible
    that they may choose the way
    to live and be creative
    and free with all due rights;

we'll fight to see a world
where differences are praised,
that no one shall go hungry
or from jobs turned away,
we'll fight to humanize
our liberating process
    that we may thus become
    more loving than our hopes;

and if we really think,
we'll END our fighting someday
and learn to live in peace,
but peace can only come
when we've resolved our envies
    and buried all our hates,
when we've decided fully
to love, to care, to sing.

    I am no threat to you
      if you're no threat to me,
and if we share the world
all people can be free.

just after taking
our Rikárd & Libertad
& their cousin, Ronnie,
for a Christmas Eve
movie & a lobster/steak dinner,
12-24-76 11 p.m.

Un PIENSASENTIMIENTO PARA
María Teresa Silva Sánchez

loved and cherished compañera,
twelve years
have we shared
feeling and thinking, living
as a unity of understanding/love,
experiencing
lo bueno y lo doloroso,
sometimes celebrating
while other times
jointly in lament,
yet, always
aware
of each other, and ever
striving
to create
within our family
a sense
of life's majesticness . . .

hoy,
con sentimiento navideño
te vuelvo a saludar,
a felicitar,
a darte
una vez más
un cantogrito poético
cual

te declama
the love i hold for you,
Teresa,
and in so doing
nos miro
dentro
the beauteous circle
of our
consanguinity,
i celebrate joyously
the belleza of our beings

within the harmony of our love . . .
felices páscuas de navidad, cariño . . .

been gone from home
almost two months
recuerdo lo pasado
y sueño futuros
3-4-77

—solo & with remembrances—

      poetically
would words flow,

      ay, before
      a walkway
de flores del desierto
before
a fireplace
would we bask then
in warmth
and tender sharing
con gentle strength
& swaying beauty—

the flames
would dance
and shadows
      on your face
would promenade,

      mujer morena paseña
      que conmigo
      doce años
      haz compartido . . .

it is evening,
wisconsin briskness
chimes out
solitude and feelings,
I walk

111

into midnight's
amorphous quietude,
aloneness cushions
the soles
of ice-cold boots,
I walk
Milwaukee streets,
          hum/sing
and realize
that life
will churn
as ever
it has churned.
yes, let us laugh,
you there, me here
wherever we can be,
ay, let us smile
& just create
from our moot time
a space
that breathes our
gentle/strong caressing
realizations,
you swim
in mine
while I
in yours
shall firmly/tenderly
immerse
the power
and
the fragileness
of all my being.

poetically/frenetically
would
all
that we speak

flow,
shadows
from firelight
upon you

they would dance,
they'd promenade
and celebrate
while feasting
on your beauty
and I'd caress
lo exquisito
of all
your you-ness
with fingertips,
strong hands,
tongue/lips,
deep vision,
& fibrous manhood
of my being. . . .

"fragrance petals its presence ..."

I. fragrance
     petals
     its presence
     onto
     realization;
     love
     is
     that
     which
     permeates
     life
     with meaning. . . .

       II. you slide
          almost quiveringly
          into my arms,
          your heated aroma
          engulfs me,
          you
          blossom, woman,
          while
          liquidly
          devouring
          my tongue,
          time
          cannot exist
          while
             we pulsate—
          one within
          the other,
          your breathing
          is quick

and then slow,
builds up
and implodes
while
my essence
explodes
inside you,
each time is new,
each time a rebirth,
ay, yes,
you loosen up
then clasp me,
your eyes dilate
as sexuality
becomes
another shaking
of our earthiness. . . .

III.

streets filled
with swaying people
proud women
dance before my gaze,
all their womanliness
glides
palatably before my vision;
veils of hunger
dissolve
while mentally/spiritually
sexual games
promenade within,
no reservations hide
within
thoughtfeelings,
only awareness
of movement
and what movement
can portend . . .

from "—torticas a la nichis—"

"let us not pretend . . ."

let us not pretend
that freedom
can be enclosed
nor defined
by fearful minds
too petty
and envidious
to realize
the beauty & power
which exist
in every living thing;
if women are to have
the dignity of liberation
they shall be the ones
to create it by
the meaning of their struggles;
if raza is to become
a sovereign people
we shall be the ones
to create our meaning,
and if
there is to be
a humanizing vitalism
it shall come
when we've all resolved
that all living things
are sacred in their being,
that differences
when respected
make of all
a beauteous people . . .
let us celebrate
each other

in this
our wondrous
human festival,
yet,
let us also realize
that life
means living
without fears
 or reservations,
that we cannot—must not—
allow
the defiling
of our beings . . .
celebrate me
with all you are
while I revel
in the festivity

of you;
 do not fear me
as I fear you not,
let us understand
that not one of us
can reign supreme,
we're all
but frail/fragile
creatures;
each one of us
can only state
a common truth;
conception,
 gestation,
birth,
 survival,
& then death,
a fleeting timespace
which
quickly must evaporate;
 so while we live

we should attempt
to love
each
moment we partake of,
that
in our passing
we make of earth
a haven . . .
a haven
which bespeaks
the worthiness
of being,
not cowardly
nor on our knees
as slaves,
but as real persons
who do their rights
defend
and who by living do declare
they'll not oppress
nor mother earth exploit. . . .

from "—tóricas a la nichis—"

—to a much older poet
from Sweden—

you
speak
with
words
which bespeak
studied concern
and gentleness;

you
speak
with a wisdom
of patient
scholarliness,
and
slow/complete smiles
gird
the studied strength
of your conclusions;

Ekner,
poeta de Sweden,
meticulous man,
your impeccable stances
generate
a slow warmth
which ultimately permeates
each moment
with a studied, caring
sense
of each moment
in its resoluteness & beauty.

Melk Weg—ze milky way
in amsterdam, menagerie
of locos & hipsters,
everybody loves jazz here
17 sept. 1978

"and in the desert . . ."

and in the desert
the dual-headed vision
cried out
      religious mandates,
      away from
the mountain
and far from
      the tree of life,
foolish people
sought out
doubleheaded idiocy,
needing its jive affirmations,
they queued up
wanting to score
a pint of drivel,
a gram of blindness,
a kilo of locura,
2 pounds of irresponsibility,
a gallon of innocent blood,
& a ton of lust & venomous envy,
anything
that would help them
obscure
their human responsibility
to vitally confront
their rapidly
      deteriorating world.
so
holocausts

became their way of life,
for none had acted
to create
a loving world.
ay, if some had acted
and created beauty/love
in measures
that knew
no borders—just all
of humankind—human
understanding
could have blossomed
to avert
the senseless ravages
and idiocies
of hate and war; but no,
their ideals,
like those
of all the peoples of this earth,
were duly bound
in ethnocentric lunacies . . .

"and it is joyful . . ."

and
it
is
joyful
to walk
in/out
the diversity
of sound
      and smiles
of the world's peoples,

not able
to fear confusion
as before,
only want
     to strive
          to understand
               it all,
to somehow
create those bridges
which will link
my limited mindsoul
to all those thoughtfeeling islands

     ambulating fearfully-confusedly,
to somehow
come to terms
with many nervous systems
that we might soothe & calm & fortify
each other::I reflect you::you
     reflect me::human circuity::ad infinitum . . .

—REGRESO—

"How was europe?" a friend asks,
"Suave, ese," I respond,
and then i begin to realize that . . . that short sojourn in
amsterdam was freer for me than anything else ever
experienced, no cops harassing me, no foolish questions, no,
i was left alone to my own designs, to walk and talk, to see
a world alien enough so that i could think and act without
having to defend anything; nights spent amidst banter, just
wandering about, almost falling through the blackholed
serenity of canal-strewn streets, laughing while basking in
the sounds of incomprehensible worlds. . . . Admonishments
still fly and power wielders still remonstrate, but spiritual
entelechy rescinds the hecticness of other days I mean to
live, whatsoever it may cost, and mean to live as only I can
live,

> vibrant
> 'neath the sun,
> aware
> that land is pungent,
> aware
> that i am land,
> and very much aware

that the sources of beingness come from our realizing that we
exist with the awesome right of exploring all dimensions to
our beings; that we were born to love—and love means self-
defense—and to love means to create, so now that i've
returned, i laugh at all those fears of yesterday,

> and while laughing say
> that living is the only art
> and art is but expression

123

              of human passions free,
              and freedom intertwines
              the thought
              and spirit's feelings
      for i saw human freedom
      spiritually unite
      a retinue of peoples
      who shared in poetry
                          i felt and heard
                          communion
                          in unison sing out

that human differentials make of us human beings, [and] now . . .

      my canto is my freedom,
      my grito is my passion,
      my poems are but extensions
      of all that i call life. . . .

"death of the body shall come …"

death of the body shall come
           soon enough
but eternity
is as near
as the pulse of poetry
written
on the quicksilver pages
of the moment's reawakening,

soy simplemente
lo que siempre seré:
           hombre entelequiado . . .

"convicts, inmates, & felons too . . ."

convicts, inmates, & felons too,
behind those shuffling feet
and vagueness in the eye
exist worlds yet to be explored;

mine and tap those hidden reservoirs,
flower, my friends, and blossom forth,
let the pen
guided by your fervent minds in quest
lead you onward
to those quiviras of joyful life;

create coyote realizations and
let your city blues eviscerate,
undulate toward those spheres
where the mind can garner
meaning and loving happenstances;
the word is mighty
when it portends
a way of life which sanguinely
sings of joy and freedom,
and freedom is a responsible
existential praxis
which implicates us
in our mutual development.

in knowing you
I sing you
songs of what it can mean
to travel worlds
and to celebrate,
so write and live,

for time shall pass,
but more importantly
you shall walk those streets,
but walk them proudly/creatively
and in love
with all that life can mean to you . . .

                              gracias for everything
                         brothers in prison blues.

from "Lemon Creek Gold:
panning for a future—
An Introduction of Sorts"

"sensuous, tortuously vibrant . . ."

III.
sensuous,
tortuously vibrant,
you implode
with your nails
joyfully/painfully
caressing
me, your lips
& burning teeth
leave trails
        y escalofriantes muecas
de lo febril
de nuestros encuentros;
after many years,
we still create
aesthetic ways
to share our love
stronger & more resilient
than in our youth,
our lubricious re-encounters
now have the intimacy of love
and sharing, no longer
just the desperate groping
of two fearful-wanting-to-be-attached
lonely individuals . . .

you are so complete now
and now I no longer feel need of you,
past the realization
that love is what attracts us,
not fear nor abjectness nor
the numbness of callow juventud, ay,
mujer, I must touch you when I see you,

not from need
but from the realization
that we learned to
complete the circle of life . . .

IV.
canto
when feelings enmesh me, when
i sense
you, pueblo mío, palpitating
within my blood,
I sing you, humanity,
songs of liberation
which smile in mirth or joy,
songs which poetically declare
that regardless of circumstance
it is, netamente, beautiful to exist.

V.
I see you, tomorrow,
within the grasp of my mindsoul,
though
      you are resilient & tenuous
         (vaguely amorphous),
I see you   there
resolute and arrogant,
also loving and concerned,
it all depends
on how I want to see you,
how much I dare to struggle
to create,
and I shall dare
to be
greater than my most creative utterance,
that word
might
flow

from
deed,
   that all my shadows be
but reflections of my self,
I embrace you
without reservation
yet aware
that if I must battle do with you
it will be quick
   and to the finish
for I've no fear
   of strangeness,
just a curious will
that sings and howls
to all the winds
that I was born to live and thrive;
my tracks
shall be among the many
who also dared to be
whatever they desired . . . if

      I am
      still alive
      tomorrow
      I shall
      sing
      a greater song
      than any
      I have sung before,

and if death
shall be my coverlet instead,
I shall then sing
as great a song
as ever I could sing,
for I have lived
as fully as I could
in barrios, prisons,
academe,
and marriage bed;
oh, I have drunk

and supped
and made of glorious love,
      so,
          let it be as much as it can be,
          until I die
          I'll merely live and ravel,
and in my way
fling out my canto
to celebrate
          the world's life.

from "—and within the vísperas—"

The University of Utah
Chicano Studies, Building 41
Salt Lake City, Utah

14 de febrero de 1980

Teresa,
en este día amoroso,
    when I think of you
deep within all that I can be,
    cantos become
your smiles
    and caresses flow
into all
    that can be defined
    as life;

years have danced
us into
    the joy
of realizing
that love is sharing,
    and we have shared
much
and created love,
    life is meaningful
and you have helped
    make each moment
    of sharing
a heartfelt singularity
which is paradisaical & harmonious,

    happy valentine's day, cariño. . . .

Festival of Children

wondrous children,
beautiful and vibrant,
     you are the songs
     swimming in my mind,
      you jump and run,
       curiously seeking
answers
to more questions
than any adult can envision.
your why is this? why is that?
can elephants really
dance
upon the head
of a pin?
oh and ah
and even ha ha ha,
but
you go on and on,
exploring
all you can,
and in doing
all you do
you make this world
a joyous place
when
you smile out of knowing
that love
surrounds
your every waking moment.

can you dance, child,
or skip rope

upon the rays
beaming down
      from a cheesy moon?
can you see
within
the skin and rinds of melons
that life
is a delicious slice
of happiness
when all goes well with you?

          and what do you silently wish for
          when it is cold outside and you
          are lying deep in your bed?
      what is the song
      you wish to sing
      as morning arrives
      to steer you on your way
      to school?

who are those things
gliding on clouds,
      can you make clouds move and sway?
and when the television shows
have gone away,
when the games have ended for the day,
oh, when cooking smells
have lifted up your sights
to soar
into the honeyed accents of your parents,
yes, holidays appear
one after the other,
and when you start to think
that someday soon
you, too, shall be grown up,
you'll have to work
to eat and clothe yourselves,
it'll be a different kind of world
where work is work

and play is something
for the weekend, if at all,
but now, oh, children,
you have this day

        in which
        to sing and jump and run,
        a day to celebrate
        the beauty of your beings,
        a day to fill your minds
        with joys,

            day dreams,

                reflections,

        and much knowledge,
        a day
        wherein
        you'll learn more
        of how to be
        the most magnificent
        you
        that
        you
        can
        be . . . you
        are
        the
        festival of life.

early morn coffee shop,
hamburgered breakfast
and art rap; Suzanne
Jamison, you are damn
good people, and
you truly care and want
to create
a better world . . . am
leaving this land today,
also finally leaving
those dreams I once had
about coming to what I
felt was my home, realize
that it is merely the home
of my ancestors; my home
shall ever exist
just beyond every horizon
I encounter, I really
don't have a land that
is mine and I might just
not even have a people
to contain me and my
soulmind's questings . . . .
en route to Albuquerque,
Belén, El Paso, San Antonio,
and then Austin, Tejas
24 de Octubre de 1981

"Manolo, carnal . . ."

Manolo, carnal,
we share
              food
                     and
                            drinks,
smoke a bit,
speak
orgiastically
of life,

finally
are we becoming
brothers
    on the outskirts
        of Belén,
yes,
Nolo,
after many years,
you
ever the oldest
of the brothers
in the family,
finally
we share
ideas, motivations,
and more than words,
we drink and sing,

and plan
reunions,
vibrantly
we part,
I go on
toward
El Paso and then Austin,
you
stay on in Belén;
years ago
when
the Navy discharged you
after World War II,
you studied music/singing
at Juilliard
in the Big Apple,
sophisticated Nolo,
you were a très chic Chicano
in a 1950s El Paso,
a city too small
        and rustic

to appreciate
a meskin
who read Whitman
          and sang
in semi-operatic tonalities,
you dressed too well,
your artist mind
was too developed
for a city
too infested
          with terse fears . . .

"con amor y cariño ..."

con amor y cariño,
in the beautifying heat
of human realization,
palabras of all hues
which embrace and caress
      a multi-hued humankind,
ay, a dance which moves
in the unison of ideals,
art forms which bespeak
that we all
on planet earth exist,
with love and concern
we embrace
      your humanity . . . . .

thoughts assail, it
becomes singular night,
pensive mood, aloneness
within Ostión multitudes . . .
Austin, Texas
15 de abril de 1983
c-s

"as we walk . . ."

                    as we walk
through the valleys
of our insecurities,
we shall act
the only way we can,
our visions
but the sum
of hope
agglutinated
to experience,
carrying the seeds
& baggage
of culture, history,
and need,
                    striving to be
all that we can be,
surviving cliches
& stereotypic images,

so that we realize
that movements
are born
as people are born,
each to live out
its moment
and impart a legacy
as rightful as any legacy
and as incorrect

as all human conjectures
about the workings
of the universal chaos,
we
are
all
just human-frail-beings,
seekers of greatness
while still fearing
the simplest
          unknowable facets
of our human-social
          vital-forces,
glorious beings
amassing data
to precisely define
our minutiae of wisdom
while we glorify
our awesome ignorance,
still, beautiful sensual
and spiritual beings,
sexual, mental,
and hysterically
intellectual—each one
crusading
for a limited
embrace with destiny;
ay, yes, let us dance
and celebrate, and then
let us undress
and explore all
we truly can be
so that we can cross
beyond all our horizons,
it is, after all,
a knowable universe
          (we hope!)
if only in bits & sketches,
and there exists

much more time than life
       (we say),
so let us celebrate
the only freedoms
we can create. . . .

from "Questions::
Moot/Salient or
Refractions. . ."

thoughts assail, it
becomes singular night,
pensive mood, aloneness
within Ostión multitudes . . .
Austin, Texass
15 de abril de 1983
c-s

"the door is open . . ."

the door is open . . .
the invitation there,
a smile engages the spirit
while the mind conjures up
a million reasons
why one shouldn't taste
the nectar of the gods;
funny
but an animal will eat
when hunger growls
in its innards
while we strive to justify
a morality
which binds us to our hungers. . . .

from "Questions::
Moot/Salient or
Refractions. . ."

730 W. Elsmere
San Anto
July 25, 1985

I Know You by Your
Smile-filled Songs, Chinto

I.
Jacinto-Temilotzín,
you arrived
within our lives
when clouds
kept the sun from view.

your first cry
broke up
darkening patterns,
a song wafted
over our landscapes . . .

II.
in Salt Lake City, Chinto,
you would pull me by the hand,
down Truman Avenue
'til we could cross State;

inside that monument
to hectic Amerika,
you would smile at the Denny's waitresses,
ask in song-filled voice
for fries and a coke,
never knowing
that such places
are usually anathema
to my quests for beauty . . .

III.
I recall those little books
you would make,
cutting papers
into tiny one-inch pages,
gluing them together,
and then writing
miniature verses
and childhood caricatures;
joyously did I read you
as I saw images dance
through your smile-filled
serenades to life . . .

IV.
I know you, Chinto,
through your human delicacy,
as your inquisitive senses
peruse all notions of the universe,
I know your anxious voice
wafting
through bookstores and galleries
your smile floats
about books and paintings,
your voice demanding
of countless poets
to proclaim
a beauty beyond the ken
of societal keepers of the keys
I know you through a love-filled family,
you running about
sweaty and juvenile
caring only about enjoyment,
asking serious questions
about death and heart attacks,
digging into familial lore
with a pungent seriousness
caught somewhere

between a daring laughter
and a joyous hope for understanding . . .

V.
more than just know you, Chinto,
I sense you everywhere
as you explore Paperbacks—y más:
nine-year-old wizard,
you take customers by the hand
and then convince some
to buy the things
you feel are valuable . . .

VI.
there probably is no need
to tell you or your sister
that you are loved, nor
need we remind Rikárd
that he, too, is loved;
 you three know
the power of embraces
as well as the beauty
of familial kisses—we
only say it
because it is our greatest truth:
the only truth worth knowing
is the one bespeaking love . . .
still, Chinto, I must again admit
that I love
that you which
swims in smile-filled songs. . . .

Jefita

Sefy would go out and sit on the concrete fence with Pete, and they would then jam with one another, going from rancheras bien deaquellas to corridos and baladas. Pete would switch moods and fly into a farruca, playing the hard high brittle notes with a sureness undergirded by love and art, and Sefy would then drop into an accompaniment of chords and bass, segundiando a brother lost in reveries of other lands where death was a common expletive, a slipping here or there.

Sometimes la Jefita would get her Gibson and walk out into the patio, her loving hands would strum and then participate. La fiesta started, the family drank and joked. There would be music, cultura in the making. We were familia, regardless of our stations. . . . .

There were no stars that night, or at least none that I would ever recall. It was a border night, the kind where the air feels static, and the sky is vast and dark, while the moon seems to dominate everything as it glides across the ebony night . . . a huge, round glaring light. . . . It felt awry as my leaden hands and wilted arms brushed against the earlier ebbing of life.

The word formed slowly and laboriously upon the mind's esophagus, struggled mightily to take off from a bewildered, broken tongue. . . . I felt the shards and sharpened syllables gnash against the spirit's ectomorphic skeins, as I saw again the eyes closing while a tear slid down my face to drop gently upon her cheek, and still did the word founder, trying desperately—maniacally—to form and then explode lovingly, to tell this wondrous and loving woman again and again that I loved her . . . she knew it, but I was anxious to say it, to shout it above the din of a world awash in gimmicks and contrivances, with the plastic notions of apple pied-coweyed evervation of convention and deformation.

Her skin was fast cooling, as the murmurs of sisters and niece plaintively asked furtive questions . . . I could not really respond . . . I saw the fingers, which had once strummed a Gibson, playing Augustín Lara compositions as her dancing eyes paraded through a 1940s E.P.T. with flair . . . she was a beautiful woman, who moved with delicacy and exuberance.

Her smart high heels accentuated a voluptuous understanding with all lifeforces as she simply went about her life, aware of the magical attraction of her being. She had been a flappergirl sixty years before, and now she was the tree of life from which generations sprang, singing her praises.

Her head rested in my arms as mortal healers tried to revive a heart which had once rejuvenated a world. The veins stood out for a final time, then became barely-visible lines traced by my eyes as I saw the pleas in the family women cutting the air with urgent pain-seared questions. . . . My hands registered the ebbing; everything else was static, even the rustle of others milling, lowing ancient paeans and keening the finality of the tree, as the branches began to waltz away into other worlds. I closed the lids gently, felt the face which had been greater and brighter than any sun or star. The lips were sealed. Never again would birdwords glide out to enchant and celebrate a vital brevity. I wanted to hear manito nuances dance through my child's mind, years ago, in the paradise of caressive love where all is understood and welcome. . . .

Inside it still seethed, struggling to break through the morass and make sense of the madness . . . the prodigal poet sought a prodigal poem, a caressive store of nouns and adjectives, verbs and nuances, only to become entrapped by a wandering potpourri of images and recollections.

Brief vignettes leapt from the bony, arthritic hands. I saw her etched on the mind's canvas . . . "¡Edúquense," Lena would gently admonish, "para que no tengan que lavarle la ropa a los gringos!" ["Get an education, so that you won't have to wash clothes for the gringos!"] Her strong, sinewy hands had washed and ironed, slaved and created. . . . Age had merely slowed her down, but her indomitable spirit was still a sprite at 81. It had not wavered at all, not even during those last 30 days at the ICU as the machine encased her body. . . .

Lena had known that city with diffidence and with artful confidence as she marched forcefully into the Catholic elementary school and confronted wearisome nuns. I saw her make the nuns apologize for terrorizing a fearful child, and the world became a wondrous blending of strength from Lena coalescing with the power of Pedro::see the tomb marker, she told the sullen, returned excon. The words spoke of a wife and son paying tribute to a loving Pedro, as her tears commingled with the prodigal pinto numero trece's prodigal tears. . . .

There was no nuance which would give sense to a senseless world, no syllables could unite to paint a portrait of a Lena able to weave stories about Chimayo just as she did. It was a livable, palatable drama ensuing . . . it was life ebbing away, leaving a palpable residue of years and tears, laughter and banter skimming palms and arms as the breathing stopped, the eyes blocked out the light and a wave of air flew by my face while I cryingly traced the face::the fine chiseled nose, the gentle lips and the sunken cheeks disappearing into images burnt into my mind's eyes.

. . . . Pedro loved you, Lena, knowing that you were truly a lovely being, a sensual being able to bring fire from the very rocks. You walked with a sentient smile upon your hips, making each moment a song of celebration—you were so festive, so lovely. Now I saw the brittle masque of human termination, as years slid upon the family face::I gently disengaged my arms, stood and uttered stones, boulders, mountains of sound into the caverns of my being. Your head burrowed deeper into the pillow as I left the room, feeling the weight of the universe . . . the barking of pending poetics and bookstore politics barged into each moment and space, creating new spaces while Lena, you marched into a corner of my mindsoul as I buried you into the hollows of new ventures.

The word which gnashed my spirit's tongue now nestles in the sweetness of remembrance. There are no flowers I can give you . . . There are only space and recollection, vignettes which dance about when the universe is gathered in by ancient, noble hands. . . . Sometimes I close your eyes and turn to speak to eyes of family, to softly say, "Yes, La Jefita is dead," yet I feel the years still living and I sometimes take the road home when visiting El Paso only to remember the moon has erased the road and El Paso no longer has streets to call me back.

lo tuyo, pueblo, es lo tuyo . . .
un ensueño,
otra posibilidad. . . .
751 Kentucky
La Oreja, Te(de)jas
[June] 1988

".... there is only one race ..."

. . . . there is only one race, one epochal people, multihued and polylinguistic—all moving through imagery and stereotype; the blade cuts through the phrase forming at the tip of the tongue gracing the delicate cuntal lips, the aroma entices while the languid folds of humanity dilate, inflate, deflate and shift like earthen plates crevicing the planet's surface, the opening and closing entrap the lingual tenacity of my spirit as Rimbaud and Verlaine collide, and cynical banter ripples the surface of human dialogue, only to dematerialize while the sunlight breaks through the clouds, and hatred makes another hasty, fearful retreat . . . .

from "Les Suerostraats
of Big Cotulla"

damn, but it's seminar and teacher
training time, el paso community
college, a collage of inane
questions & other insipid
modalities; it's fun to see them
go through their paces, jump,
rover, hump . . .

—words—

spastic & droning words,
heat amidst
mechinistic role playing,
ay, drowning
in an insensate morass
as death
stalks us
in our societal idiocy;

learning
how
    to
       institute
order
       into the beautiful chaos
of feelings
so that
even in our seeing beauty/life
do we teach
one another
to mechanically define
a vitality
killed
    by the one-two-three
       objectification
    of schooling . . .

let
us
march
forward
       onward
into the sterile labyrinths
of a pedagogical nightmare,
grasping gears & pedals,
narrowing experience,
and celebrating bland-ness,

hut   two   three   four
let us close our minds once more.

....There is only
the open door ..."

.... There is only the open door, a gateway pointing West or East, maybe North,
but the heart bleeds in rhythmic cadence as the caliche breaks off the barrio walls,
the peeling paint is ancient and the new too damn new, the coating on the verbs
and nouns has too much of another era, another place, and the lyrics speak to a
world abounding with Chicano salsa beats, a harmonic sensibility building to a
crescendo which might overpower the horrid panic awaiting his and her
amerikanisms, barbaric toledo steel or clinical german scalpels, they all lance the
same:: it's all existential as we reflect each other:: our hands roam flesh and share
fulfillment, we eat of each other,

     querida-in-your-many-hues,

     I love us as we coincide again and again, our many facets dance and
celebrate, each meeting too short and fleeting:: sunlight graces you in your many
splendours, your bronzes and ebonies, your alabaster and olive, your redolence and
amaranth, oh, golden tawny strains, we merge and sing upon the plains of human
destiny:: we ride each other, love, and wash the guilt with human nectars, assuaged
we dance upon the cityscapes, moving to the conga electronic beat:: cacaphony sings
your names, my poet's tongue glides into your salient valleys, seeking the nectar and
the power of all life; you implode raking nails upon my mind as my soul pirouettes
through our birthing sensibilities:: unfold, enfold and gyrate, we rise through the
fog and entangle our limbs on earthen wonder as my eyes roam you/devour pan
dulce and pretzel womanity,

     no, I do not want to own you nor can I, my power is too fragile and too
evanescent to pretend that you are less or that you can fit in my pocket beside my
cigarette pack:: you, too, are a giant, an amorphous being of many silhouettes and
nuances, and I cannot possibly fit in your pocketbook! no! we both merely fit in
the bosoms and hollows of an earthen ball glazed by a gaseous energizer:: and we fit
into one another when we realize ourselves, oh, yes, I love us, this moment in its
miraculous being what it is:: the wind caresses us as a whirling, churning globe skirts
the edges of the universe and we gaze in wonderment, fighting all the insecurities we
straddle ourselves with, let us hold each other and offer prayer to the earth and sun,
to the resilience of your skin as you envelop the stamen of my word::

drink, cariño, my nectar
as I lap your budding cuntal walls:: let us be joy singing of human mystery and
creation, let your soft tongue break hardness that mine might create a poem upon
the river of your humanity, and as we feed our human senses we will create the
plasma to keep the world sane and loving:: we are not beasts nor things, we are . . . .

*from "Les Suerostraats
of Big Cotulla"*

"Female form . . ."

Female form
ultra modernistic,
     futuristic/traditional
     fusing
of powers; light
filters through
amber glass eye
among
            sunflower/maguey
                 foliage;
adobe walls
and stair walkway
where miniature
ceramic basset face
guards
passageway; I walk
gingerly/excitedly
upon human earthen
facts of empowerment,
feel the shaman song
emanating
from indigenous being
sprouting through
clay-cement
of our humanity—
a song to life
wails
as stark imagery
dances
freely

with nuance, oh, yes,
Mago
becomes dervish art-cum-artist
on the gentle September heat
of Tonatiuh
gracing a bordered understanding
while explosive sounds
drum in the distant desert;
it is Chihuahua, Tejas, Nuevo Mexico
fusing elements in humanizing clay,
as monumental miniature bronzes
grace
a garden
    on Cui—

—poema a Rie ét Rik y luv—

a.

within that Sánchez
sense of the universe,
a familial swirling world
basking in New Mexican
understandings merged
with El Pasoan sensibility,
oh, from our people
born to the power of
sunlight defining
our world, we greet you,
o lovely and vibrant
Rie Nakai, and embrace
your becoming wife and
pillar, support and love,
wise and life-giving
woman also from a land
where the sun is a song
to meaning and tradition . . .

b.

we welcome you, Rie Nakai,
to be as one with our family,
and we enjoy even
the music of your name:
Rie in español/Spanish
means "to laugh,"
laugh in a most pleasing
sense of language, of being
human and natural, to nurture
joy and festivity.

Nakai, in the Native American
world of the wondrous Navajo
means "Mexican,"
and it is a joy to know
that in languages other
than your own lovely Japanese
I will think joyously of my
new daughter as
Rie Nakai Sánchez, o yes,
Laughs Mexican Sánchez . . .

c.

mi'jo, my son Rikard,
you enter into beauty
and human realization
as you merge your humanity
that of love Rie Nakai,
and it is your honor that
will be shared between
you both, that your two
families might celebrate
a new beginning, a joy our
sense of the world
unfolding with delicacy
such as we festively
admire in the blossoms
of flowers and fruit
of nature sustaining us,
o you enter into meaning
to create a new history . . .

d.

may the family of Rie Nakai
welcome you, our dear son,
that there might flow
a loving kindness amongst
all, and though we will
be away from this moment

where sunlight and joy
commingle to create
new songs of being and love,
we send spiritual embraces
to both that the world
might somehow stop
to find meaning
in the joyous love shared
by two young people
crossing the oceans
of culture and histories
to create a new sensibility
sensitive to possibility,
we love you both . . .

Los Sánchez

About the Author

Ricardo Sánchez (1941-1995) is considered one of the fathers of the Chicano literary genre and is one of the most published and anthologized Chicano writers. His family had roots in northern New Mexico for more than five generations, but moved to El Paso, Texas, before his birth. Sánchez was raised in a tough neighborhood of El Paso. Inquisitive, intelligent, and streetwise, he felt stunted by the insensitive school system of the 1950s and dropped out. He later obtained a GED and in 1969 received a Frederick Douglass Fellowship in Journalism and wrote for an African-American newspaper in Richmond, Virginia. In 1970 he worked as a staff writer and humanities instructor at the University of Massachusetts, Amherst. In 1974, Sánchez earned a PhD in American studies and cultural linguistic theory from the Union Graduate School in Cincinnati, Ohio. He taught at El Paso Community College, New Mexico State University in Las Cruces, University of Wisconsin at Milwaukee, University of Alaska, and Washington State University. At WSU he achieved full professorship with tenure.

He traveled continuously throughout the United States, lecturing and reading at many universities and poetry festivals. He also was invited to the Poets of the Latin World in Mexico City and the One World Poetry Festival in Amsterdam. He conceived and co-founded the Canto al Pueblo Festival. His papers are archived at the University of Texas at Austin and at Stanford University. Information on Sánchez is accessible via the Internet at <http://www.dr-ricardo-sanchez.com>.

OTHER WORKS BY RICARDO SÁNCHEZ

Canto y grito mi liberacion/The Liberation of a Chicano Mind Soul. El Paso, Texas: Míctla Publications, 1971. Garden City, New York: Anchor Books, Doubleday & Co., 1973. Pullman, Washington: WSU Press, 1995 (expanded edition with "Canto II").

HECHIZOspells. Los Angeles: Chicago Studies Center/Publication Unit, University of California at Los Angeles, 1976.

Milhaus Blues and Gritos Norteños. Milwaukee, Wisconsin: Spanish-Speaking Outreach Institute, University of Wisconsin, 1978.

Brown Bear Honey Madness: Alaskan Cruising Poems. Austin, Texas: Slough Press, 1981.

Selected Poems. Houston, Texas: Arte Público Press, 1985.

Eagle-Visioned/Feathered Adobes. El Paso, Texas: Cinco Punto Press, 1990.

American Journeys::Jornados Americanas. Iowa City, Iowa: Rob Lewis, Publisher, 1994.